WALKING IN THE LIGHT

Walking In The Light

ROY CLEMENTS

EASTBOURNE

Biblical quotations are from the
New International Version © International Bible Society
1973, 1978, 1984. Published by Hodder & Stoughton

Front cover photo: Tony Stone Photolibrary—London

British Library Cataloguing in Publication Data

Clements, Roy
  Walking in the light.
  1. Bible. N.T. John—Critical studies
  I. Title
  226'.506

ISBN 0-86065-540-7

Printed in Great Britain for
KINGSWAY PUBLICATIONS LTD
1 St Anne's Road, Eastbourne, E Sussex BN21 3UN by
Richard Clay Ltd, Bungay, Suffolk.
Typesetting by
Nuprint Ltd, 30b Station Road, Harpenden, Herts AL5 4SE

Contents

	Preface	7
Chapter 1	Life (1 John 1:1–4)	9
Chapter 2	Light (1 John 1:5–2:2)	27
Chapter 3	The World (1 John 2:3–17)	45
Chapter 4	The Lie (1 John 2:18–27; 4:1–6)	61
Chapter 5	Holiness (1 John 2:28–3:10)	77
Chapter 6	Love (1 John 3:11–18; 4:7–12; 4:19–21)	95
Chapter 7	Confidence (1 John 3:19–24; 4:13–18)	117
Chapter 8	Faith (1 John 5:1–21)	137
	Notes	153

Preface

One of the most important challenges facing Christians today is that of maintaining the balance between mind and heart in our spirituality. A tension between doctrine and experience, Word and Spirit, charismatic and evangelical is plain to see. This is what makes the first letter of John particularly relevant. The apostle too was concerned about preserving this balance in a church where it was in danger of being lost. My sincere hope is that this series of printed sermons will help to highlight the issues involved so that all who share a common commitment to 'the Father and the Son' (1 Jn 2:24) may 'love one another' (1 Jn 4:7) and 'keep themselves from idols' (1 Jn 5:21).

The addresses that comprise this book were preached at Eden Baptist Church in Cambridge during 1981. Little has been done to the transcripts to prepare them for publication. They remain substantially as they were preached. Thanks are owed to those whose diligence prepared typescripts and edited them from the original tape recordings, especially Mrs Pat Blake, Chris Akhurst and Paul Riddington.

1 John is really a rhapsody on a number of related themes which keep re-emerging. At times this makes it difficult to expound in a consecutive way. Readers who

wish to use the book as an aid to their own Bible study should note that several of the later chapters of the book overlap in the sections of the letter they are expounding.

Finally a word of gratitude to Christopher Catherwood of Kingsway for his personal encouragement in getting these sermons into print.

Roy Clements

Chapter 1

Life

1 John 1:1–4

> Doctrine? Oh no, we don't want doctrine! It is so divisive,
> spoiling the harmony of our fellowship. Doctrine is so
> complicated. It obscures the simplicity of our testimony.
> It is so stuffy too, suffocating the way we express our joy.
> No, we don't want doctrine, all those theoretical ideas
> when what we want is reality. Doctrine is just bookish
> intellectualism but we want experience. Doctrine is just
> dead orthodoxy; we want life!

Sentiments like these have been expressed with such
monotonous regularity and with such widespread support
over the last twenty years that they have become part of
the conventional wisdom of some Christian groups. Doctrine, if not quite a dirty word, is certainly regarded as a
tedious irrelevancy in many circles. Christians who seek to
swim against the tide and campaign for doctrinal norms in
the church are often disparaged as misguided reaction-
aries who are frustrating the movement of the Holy Spirit
in our day towards unity and renewal.

That is why a careful study of 1 John is not just desirable for Christians today but absolutely imperative. Surprising as it may seem, precisely the same kind of
controversy about the importance of doctrine was

developing in the church at the end of the first century as
now characterises the church at the end of the twentieth.

Gnosticism

A group of false teachers was emerging. They wanted to
cut loose from the structure of orthodox Christian teaching which the church had been built upon in its early
days. In particular, they were embarrassed by the doctrine of the Incarnation. The Christmas story for them
was not just a miracle but an impossibility. According to
their philosophy, matter and spirit, like oil and water,
could never mix. They were incompatible, polar
opposites: matter was essentially evil and spirit was essentially good. So God who obviously was a spirit, could
never really become flesh, at least not in the crude and
literal sense which the early Christians suggested. Such an
idea was for them, quite literally, unthinkable.

These false teachers thought that the early Christians
must somehow have got it wrong, which was understand-
able since the apostles were unsophisticated and unedu-
cated Jewish peasants. What really happened must have
been rather different and these false teachers, armed with
their superior philosophical insight, had plenty of alternative suggestions to offer.

Perhaps, they suggested, God's spirit just manifested
itself in the shape of a human being for a while like a
phantom. Jesus had an outward appearance that seemed
like a material body, but on close examination it would
have been revealed to have been insubstantial, weightless
and ethereal. Alternatively, if that were not the case,
God's spirit just occupied a certain human body for a
while like a ghost haunting a house. There was of course
nothing divine about the particular man, who conven-
iently acted as host in this way; Jesus was just an ordinary
human being in whom the spirit dwelt temporarily.

We do not have to speculate about the currency of these erroneous first-century ideas. The first one was called Docetism and the second was associated with a man called Cerinthus. Together they formed part of an extremely complex heresy called Gnosticism.

It may seem surprising that two completely different theories of who Jesus was, the Docetic and that of Cerinthus, could be characteristic of the same heresy. Yet, for the gnostics, precise theological definition was really unimportant. All kinds of mutually contradictory ideas seasoned the soup of gnostic speculation, for Gnosticism was not a religion of revealed truths, but a religion of mystical enlightenment.

Like some Christians in the twentieth century, the gnostics did not want doctrine, but life, and that for them meant knowing how to have esoteric experiences in the spiritual realm, rising above the physical plane to make contact with heavenly powers beyond this material universe. In fact, Gnosticism had a lot more in common with Theosophy, or with Hinduism, than it did with authentic Christianity. What you believed was really insignificant, because it was the experience of mystical enlightenment that marked you out as a spiritual person.

All this was quite different of course from the gospel which the apostles had preached. Unfortunately, by the end of the first century, almost all the apostles had died. How, therefore, were these threatening denials of the reality of the Incarnation going to be opposed in the absence of men who could speak out with first-hand knowledge of Christ in the flesh?

There was in the providence of God just one hope, a sole surviving contact with the apostolic age: John, the son of Zebedee, who once by the Sea of Galilee had been personally summoned by Jesus to discipleship. By now he was a very old man, living in Ephesus in Asia Minor. In earlier years he seems to have written very little; certainly nothing has come down to us from his pen which is contemporary with the earlier writing of Mark, or Luke, or Paul.

It seems to have been the infiltration of these false gnostic teachers at the very end of the first century that provoked him into becoming an author, probably for the first time. For both his great Gospel and his three letters, bear the same stamp of a theological concern to refute gnostic opinion. Certainly tradition confirms that, in his later years, John was an outspoken opponent of this particular heresy.

There is one rather humorous story that has come down to us from the church historian, Irenaeus. He tells us how on one occasion the aged John entered the public baths in Ephesus, presumably to have a nice refreshing dip before lunch. No sooner had he gone through the door, than he observed the gnostic Cerinthus already there in the baths. Whereupon the old man rushed from the building in a theatrical display of horror and feigned panic. 'Quick,' he said, 'run for your lives. The bathing house is about to fall down. Cerinthus, the enemy of truth, is inside!'

Doctrine mattered to John

Unlike the gnostics, and unlike some of our twentieth-century Christian contemporaries, John believed that doctrine mattered enormously.

Firstly, it was vital in the area of Christian morals, because our beliefs condition our behaviour. Gnosticism, as we shall see in due course, had a devastating effect on people's attitude to sin.

More than that, it was essential to John in the area of Christian unity, for without a clearly defined confession of faith on which to build her common life, the church inevitably disintegrates into factions. Gnosticism, again as we shall see later, gave rise to a most regrettable lovelessness and a super-spiritual elitism in the church.

Thirdly, doctrine mattered to John for the sake of Christian evangelism, because doctrine is what makes Christianity distinctive. It is what lifts it out of the amorphous sea of the multitudinous varieties of mystical experience with which Gnosticism cluttered the world, and places it uniquely on the solid bedrock of objective truth.

More important than anything else, doctrine also mattered to John because it was vital to Christian assurance. Perhaps the most wicked thing that Gnosticism did was to undermine the faith of simple believers. Many of them could not take the wholesale scepticism of orthodox Christianity which these eloquent and plausible teachers, such as Cerinthus, displayed. Humble Christian souls were shaken. They began to torment themselves with the thought: 'Perhaps I'm not saved after all. Perhaps this new gnostic movement they are all talking about has got it right and the Christianity that I have been brought up on all these years is wrong!'

John's purpose in writing

Consequently, therefore, John wrote this first letter, pre-eminently to press upon us the crucial importance of doctrine in the believer's life.

To begin with, his purpose is pastoral. He wants to counteract the confusion that these false ideas were causing in the minds of honest Christians and for that reason his words are often gentle and affectionate. He counters the moral permissiveness that they were fostering with words like these: 'My dear children, I write this to you so that you will not sin' (2:1). He rebuts the disunity they were causing with tender words like these: 'Dear friends, let us love one another' (4:7). Most of all, he continually refutes the doubts that the gnostics were sowing in the minds of some of his congregation with reassuring words like these: 'I write these things to you who believe in the name of the Son of God so that you may know that you have eternal life' (5:13).

Few letters in the New Testament breathe such a warmth of pastoral concern. On the other hand, John was determined in this letter to contradict the propaganda of these false teachers, which he saw as responsible for the moral, social and spiritual problems that were developing in the congregation. Gnosticism was not just a radical Christian movement that John was too conservative or too old-fashioned to appreciate, but a pernicious conspiracy of lies. It could not be tolerated, and so John's amiability clashes strangely with a tone of harsh and uncompromising belligerence that sometimes takes the reader by surprise:

> See that what you have heard from the beginning remains in you (2:24).
>
> Every spirit that acknowledges that Jesus Christ has come in the flesh is from God, but every spirit that does not acknowledge Jesus is not from God. This is the spirit of the antichrist (4:2,3).
>
> We are from God, and whoever knows God listens to us; but whoever is not from God does not listen to us. This is how we recognise the Spirit of truth and the spirit of falsehood (4:6).

Doctrine mattered so much to John that this gentle pastor who above anybody championed love of the brethren could when occasion demanded, become a zealous inquisitor campaigning for the excommunication of heretics.

Its significance for us

Any indifference on our part to doctrinal issues would
provoke no less indignation from John if he were alive
today. All who say, 'We don't want doctrine, we want
experience,' need to reflect on that. With such a sentiment
Cerinthus and his fellow gnostics would have heartily
concurred.

We risk being most grievously misled by contemporary
errors, just as Gnosticism misled many in the second
century, if we fail to learn from 1 John that we cannot have
Christian experience without Christian doctrine. They go
together; they are inseparable. The first letter of John is at
once a pastoral sermon and a theological tract aimed at
those who thought you could separate them.

The life revealed

> That which was from the beginning, which we have heard,
> which we have seen with our eyes, which we have looked
> at and our hands have touched—this we proclaim con-
> cerning the Word of life. The life appeared; we have seen it
> and testify to it, and we proclaim to you the eternal life,
> which was with the Father and has appeared to us (1:1,2).

This brief prologue sets the scene in many respects for
the entire letter, because it brings together the primary
doctrine and the primary experience of the Christian faith,
and defines the inseparable connection which links the
two of them together.

Those familiar with John's Gospel will detect, even in
translation, many echoes in these two verses of the opening lines of that larger work, and in fact in the original
Greek the parallels are far more obvious. Indeed, the
similarities between John 1 and 1 John 1 are so obviously
intentional that it poses a problem of interpretation for us.

Double meanings

Is the subject of these opening verses the gospel message or Jesus Christ? For instance, when John speaks of the 'Word of life' at the end of verse 1, does he mean the life-giving message which the apostles were commissioned to proclaim or is it rather a title for the life-giving Saviour, Jesus, whom in the Gospel John called 'The Word'?

Similarly, when John says, 'that which was from the beginning', does he mean, as he does in many other places in this letter (eg 2:7), the gospel as the apostles received it at the beginning in its pristine and undistorted truth? Or again, is it a reference, as in the first verses of his Gospel, to the eternal pre-existence of Christ, who was 'with God in the beginning'?

We cannot solve these ambiguities with certainty and, as a result, many scholars complain that John is abstruse and ungrammatical. Some even suggest that these words cannot have been composed by the same man who wrote the Gospel. They must be an attempt by an unknown writer to bathe in the reflected eminence of the Gospel by quoting its phraseology, but in a much more clumsy and inept fashion than the original author of the Gospel would ever have been guilty of.

However, such scholars have surely failed to observe John's penchant for double entendre. The Gospel of John is full of double meanings, word plays and enigmatic expressions. These opening verses of the epistle are just another example of that characteristic style which John uses. It is his idiosyncratic way of conveying a sense of the mystery and the profundity of the things he is talking about.

The ambiguity in the phrases 'that which was from the beginning' and 'the Word of life' is quite deliberate. John intends to confuse us as to whether he is talking about the apostolic testimony to Christ or about Christ himself because in actual fact he is talking about both. The point which he is trying to get across to us in these opening verses is that the only access we have to the one is via the other. In a sense they are not two different things in our experience. Christ and the apostolic testimony to Christ are woven together for us. The life of God in Christ can only be experienced by *us* because it was once in a particular time and place revealed to *others* who have told us about it.

'The life' revealed

So he says in verse 2: 'The life appeared; we have seen it and testify to it, and we proclaim to you the eternal life, which was with the Father and has appeared to us.'

Eternal life for John is not a commodity which a man can add to the inventory of his possessions; nor is it even, as the gnostics suggested, a kind of mystical force-field which we can plug into once we know the right spiritual techniques. Eternal life, John tells us, is a relationship with an eternal person. The picture that John is conjuring up by his choice of tense and preposition in the phrase 'which was with the Father' is that of a dynamic face-to-face relationship of ever deepening intimacy. Here is someone who shared eternity with God in a most extraordinary way. Yet he 'appeared', stepping out on to the stage of history like a light bulb being switched on after being concealed in the darkness. He who was eternal life became visible and, John says, 'We saw him.'

John's apostolic authority

John uses the first person pronoun 'we' a lot in this letter. More often than not it is used to include the author with his readers, as when he says, 'We have one who speaks to the Father in our defence' (2:1) and 'How great is the love the Father has lavished on us, that we should be called children of God!' (3:1).

Here, however, John is using that pronoun 'we' in a different way, not to include himself with his readers, but to distinguish himself from them. The contrast here is not 'we' as opposed to 'they', but 'we' as opposed to 'you': 'We have seen it and...proclaim [it] to you' (1:2). In other words, John is claiming a unique position within the church. He does this not by virtue of any special merit on his part. When it comes to the forgiveness of sins or his adoption as a child of God, he is in exactly the same boat as everybody else.

John's unique authority, he tells us, derives from two sources. First, he was an eye-witness. He was personally present at the historical manifestation of eternal life in a way that his hearers were not. Secondly, his unique authority derives from divine commission, because he was specially appointed by Christ to report this revelation to the world.

This is not then the 'we' of Christian fellowship that John is using here in verses 1 and 2 of his letter, but the 'we' of apostolic privilege. It is vital to grasp how important that is. Heresy threatens the church only when the church fails to acknowledge that distinctive authority which the apostles rightly claim as those who are personal witnesses and appointees of Christ.

When the apostles realised they were dying out, they did not point the church to some central magisterium, either in Jerusalem or in Rome, where theological controversies could be settled. They did not appoint apostolic successors in their place; nor did they encourage the church to seek the gift of inspired utterance in the congregation, to solve their doctrinal differences. They simply saw to it that the church was left with a written account of their apostolic understanding of the gospel. The answer to all questions of Christian faith and conduct lies not in

Popes, not in Councils, not in contemporary prophecies, but in the teaching of those first-generation Christians whom Christ commissioned. In a word, it lies in doctrine and apostolic doctrine in particular.

Gnosticism would be defeated at a stroke once the church gave proper weight to the apostolic books of the New Testament as God intended.

Unlike these false teachers, with their presumptuous speculations, John could say, 'We have heard it. We have received the gospel first-hand from the very lips of Christ.' He could say, 'We have seen it, not with the inner vision of mystical experience, but with our own eyes. Ours was no distant or cursory glance. We have examined this life made manifest with the closest scrutiny, with the most intense inspection, and,' says John, 'just in case you still think Galilean peasants cannot tell a ghost from flesh and blood, even when it stares them in the face, we also touched it with our hands. And our testimony to what we saw, heard and handled is this—he was no phantom. He was no spirit-possessed zombie, but eternal life incarnate. He was God made flesh to dwell among us. This,' he says, 'is the primary doctrine of the Christian faith to which we apostles testify as eye-witnesses, which we proclaim as revealed truths; God has given us eternal life by giving us himself.'

The only way you and I are going to find eternal life is by finding him who is life incarnate, and the only way we can possibly do that is by paying attention to the God-appointed testimony of those who saw and heard him. It is not mystical technique that leads us to eternal life, but the teaching of the apostles.

The life shared

We proclaim to you what we have seen and heard, so that you also may have fellowship with us. And our fellowship is with the Father and with his Son, Jesus Christ. We write this to make our joy complete (1:3,4).

I suppose there are few words more overworked in the Christian vocabulary these days than 'fellowship'. What do we mean by it? I suspect that for some of us it implies a kind of warm camaraderie generated after singing the same chorus at least a dozen times very heartily.

The Greek word, *koinonia*, means sharing, or more literally having something 'in common' with somebody else. What does John imply when he says his purpose in proclaiming the life incarnate is that his hearers should have something 'in common' with him and the other apostles? Have what in common?

It could mean they should share the gospel and we would probably have understood him to have meant that if he had not gone on to say, 'And our fellowship is with the Father and with his Son.' That rather throws a spanner in the works. It is flattering enough to imagine that we have something in common with apostles, but to suggest that we have something in common with the Trinity must be bordering on blasphemy.

What, then, can the church share with one another, the apostle John, Jesus and God the Father? The answer is really not so difficult. It is what John has been talking about all through these verses—life. That is what binds the church together, the shared experience of spiritual life. That is why Paul calls us the body of Christ. What is a body but a collection of bits of organic machinery that happen to share the same metabolism? Christians are similarly bound together as an organism with a common life, the life of God. 'For God so loved the world that he gave his one and only Son, that whoever believes in him shall not perish, but have eternal life' (Jn 3:16). That is what the gospel is all about.

Doctrine and experience

In one respect, the gnostics were absolutely right: Christianity is not just a history lesson. It is about a personal participation in eternal life, the life of God in the souls of men. The gnostics were not wrong to insist upon such an experiential dimension to the Christian religion.

For there is such a thing as dead orthodoxy and it is a travesty of what Christianity is meant to be. John would have been the first to agree that Christianity is far more than just mental assent to a creed. But, and it is most important that we grasp this, though Christianity is more than mere mental assent to a creed, it can never, never, never be less than that. The fellowship, the sharing of life, which Christianity offers flows out of our acceptance of the apostle's testimony to Jesus. That is why John says, 'We proclaim this message to you, *so that* you may have fellowship in this experience of the life incarnate with us.'

Notice the order: the experience of life is a consequence of the apostolic teaching. The two are inseparable. You cannot have the experience of Christ without the doctrine of Christ; the one is the corollary of the other.

The gnostics wanted to short-circuit that process and have eternal life direct, without any reference to historical events or to apostolic instruction. They wanted to experience the Spirit of Christ without any commitment to the Incarnation, or the Atonement, or the Resurrection. In a word, they wanted to cut Christianity free from doctrine and reduce it to just another form of oriental mysticism. A technique for expanding your consciousness, a kind of non-addictive LSD; that is what Christianity was for them. But John is saying here that you cannot do that. If you do, it is not Christianity you end up with, but something else. You cannot have the experience of Christ without the doctrine of Christ.

Contemporary 'Gnosticism'

This is a most important lesson for us to learn because it seems to me, without any exaggeration, that there is in the contemporary church in the West a definite process of what I can only call 'gnostification' going on. Let me give you three examples.

In evangelism

Increasingly when we talk about evangelism, what we have in mind is the sharing of experience, not the proclamation of doctrine. That word 'testify' that John uses in this introduction to his letter can mislead us in that regard. When we talk about a 'testimony', we mean our subjective experience of Christ, 'what Christ has done for me'. Yet when the apostle John talks about testimony, he means what his eyes had seen of Christ. If we confuse these two quite distinct kinds of testimony, inevitably what happens is that we reduce Christianity from a religion anchored in certain events that took place in history to just another form of mystical experience.

Our testimony is quite different from the apostle's testimony. Evangelism is not a matter of telling the world what God has done for us. Though that may be a very good illustration of the gospel, it is not evangelism. Evangelism is announcing what God has done in time and history before the eyes of the apostles for the world. Evangelism is concerned with proclaiming doctrine, not merely with sharing experience.

I remember once talking to some university students who were being assailed by the sect of an Eastern guru who was offering enlightenment, much as did the gnostics. I was appalled to see the way the Christians were reacting. The guru's devotees were saying, 'You should come to my spiritual master; he gives you a marvellous experience of peace and joy.' And Christians were replying, 'No,

you should come to our spiritual Master. He gives an even
better experience of peace and joy!' That was all it was, a
competition between rival experiences.

We are not reduced to that. Evangelism is not the mere
sharing of personal experience, it is the proclamation of
biblical doctrine. That is not to say that personal experience has no place. Telling people what God has done for
us will add immeasurably to the power of what we say to
them about Jesus, but we cannot substitute testimony for
evangelism. The two are different.

In theology

The gnostification of Christianity is occuring today at a
more academic level too. Over the last hundred years or
so, there has been a determined attempt by scholars to
strip away Christianity's ties to history and concentrate
instead on the subjective, experiential side of things. That
is why the category of myth has become so important to
theologians in the twentieth century. The Virgin Birth,
the deity of Christ, the return of Christ, are all part, they
say, of the mythical framework which the church created
in order to communicate and interpret her experience of
Christ.

Some have even spoken of distinguishing the Jesus of
history, who was a perfectly ordinary, unremarkable Jewish peasant, from the Christ of faith, who is a glorious life-
giving Spirit of the church's worship.

Now it would be quite improper to portray these theologians as malicious agents of Satan who are out to
destroy the church. They sincerely believe that such a
process of de-mythologising the gospel is necessary if the
gospel is to be credible to our modern scientific world. But
that is precisely what the gnostics thought they were
doing. The gnostic Cerinthus himself distinguished
between Jesus the man and Christ the eternal Spirit.

These were two different things as far as he was concerned, and John's response to Cerinthus' distinguishing between the Jesus of history and the Christ of faith was not to say, 'Well done, Cerinthus, you're doing a great job here contextualising Christianity in this Hellenistic culture of ours,' but, 'Flee the baths, the enemy of truth is within!'

There are certain limits beyond which our theological speculations may not go, no matter how sceptical the world may become, and one of those limits is that God really did walk this earth in flesh and blood. Deny the true deity and true humanity of Jesus Christ and you have denied the faith. Thinker you may be, Christian thinker you have ceased to be. And the church must have the courage to say so. You cannot have the experience of Christ in the church without the apostolic doctrine of Christ in the Bible. To try to separate these things is not Christianity at all but Gnosticism.

In worship

I value the charismatic movement for the way in which it has revived dead churches to spiritual life. No one who has the interests of God's kingdom at heart can fail to be glad at such renewal. But one of the worries that I have about that movement in some of its manifestations, at least, is that it represents a gnostification of Christian worship.

I am reminded of the man that John Stott cites. 'When I go to church, I feel I want to unscrew my head and put it under my seat,' he said.[1] In other words, worship is something that should bypass the mind. It should lift us up into a non-rational transcendental ecstasy. It should be experiential, not doctrinal.

This attitude to worship shows particularly in the hymnology of the twentieth century. Consider the choruses we sing. I enjoy singing them, but it has to be said there is

often very little doctrine in them. They are songs of experience not of teaching, and in that the charismatic revival
differs considerably from the evangelical revival of two
centuries ago. If you look at the hymns that came out of
the eighteenth century, you will see that they are
crammed full of doctrine.

For Christians in that time of revival, worship meant
intelligent adoration of a God who was known through the
teaching of the Bible. That is what they celebrated in their
hymns. For them, worship was not just an attempt to get
spiritually high, ecstatic, or emotional. It involved thinking about doctrine and I judge that the apostle John was
on their side in that.

The apostle Paul says, 'I will pray with my spirit, but I
will also pray with my mind; I will sing with my spirit, but
I will also sing with my mind' (1 Cor 14:15).

The Master himself tells us, 'When you pray, do not
keep on babbling like pagans,' a clear reference to the
unintelligible, ecstatic utterances of pagan worship (Mt
6:7). 'This...is how you should pray: "Our Father, in
heaven..."' (Mt 6:9). What is the Lord's Prayer but a
simple rational expression of Christian doctrine?

Christian worship is intelligent worship, for it is worship informed and set on fire by the truth. If we allow our
worship to degenerate into just an orgy of pious senti-
ality, we are not worshipping as Christians, but as gnostics.

The fruit of doctrine

So there are lessons of immense relevance to us at the end
of the twentieth century in 1 John. Doctrine is vitally
relevant to our evangelism, our theology, and our worship. And as we proceed through this letter, we shall find
it relevant in many other areas of Christian life too.

If we say we do not want doctrine because it is devisive and it spoils the fellowship, John tells us in these opening verses that, on the contrary, it is doctrine that creates true fellowship.

If we think we do not want doctrine because it is complicated and obscures our witness, on the contrary, John tells us that doctrine is our authentic witness.

If we insist that doctrine is stuffy and suffocates our joy, John would remind us that, properly understood, doctrine is the source of fullness of joy: 'We write this to make our joy complete' (1:4).

If we say we do not want doctrine, because we want life, John tells us that we cannot have the one without the other. Fellowship, witness, joy and life are not the opposites of doctrine, they are the fruit of it.

Chapter 2

Light

1 John 1:5–2:2

The preacher's dilemma

All things considered, the preacher's job is not an easy one. Have you thought, for instance, how difficult it is to try to meet the huge variety of needs there are in the average congregation all in the compass of a single sermon? People are so diverse. There are different age groups, backgrounds, races, levels of intelligence, degrees of maturity, circumstances of life. How can one man in one address possibly communicate to such a heterogeneous company? It is a formidable task.

Indeed, the polarisation between different individuals in the same church can be such that a sermon which is quite right for one is absolutely inappropriate and even dangerously misleading to another. Consider, for example, the question of sin in a Christian's life.

The Bible obviously takes a very serious view of God's judgement, and so it is not difficult to find texts upon which to preach powerful and challenging sermons on the necessity of Christian holiness. Yet there are some Christians for whom that kind of sermon can be very discouraging and counter-productive. These are the hyper-sensitive types, who have by nature a very high degree of anxiety in their personality, so that any little thing tends to worry them enormously. Maybe they suffer from some kind of irrational fear, like claustrophobia. They often tend to have stress-induced depressions, or are the sort that live on their nerves and need tablets to keep their emotions under control.

Most vulnerable of all to the holiness sermon are the idealistic types, people with an obsession about perfection. For them, everything must be 'just so'. They are immaculate in their home, and particularly in themselves. When you ask them to describe their own personalities, they always major on the negative things. They have 'a low self-image' and so tend to run themselves down; they look in the mirror only to count their spots or their wrinkles.

When the pastor preaches a good strong holiness sermon, this kind of over-sensitive type is invariably thrown into a guilt-ridden inferiority complex as a result. 'Oh!' they say. 'What a useless Christian I am! I have no right to call myself a Christian. Perhaps I am not one at all. Perhaps I have committed the unforgivable sin. Look at brother X or sister Y—so spiritual, so capable. That is what a Christian should be like. I am not, nor could I ever be like that. No, the pastor is right; Christians should be holy and I am miserably unholy. I might as well give up pretending. I am a hypocrite—that's all.'

Of course, that is not the reaction the pastor wanted, but those who are inclined to anxiety almost inevitably overreact in that way to the solemn warnings and the lofty standards with which his holiness sermon is liberally seasoned. Their guilt feelings are, needless to say, quite out of proportion to any real sin in their lives, but in spite of that, their assurance of salvation is dashed and a dark despair falls over them. That sermon was very necessary for some, no doubt, but it had the most undesirable side effects on these hypersensitive souls.

In contrast to that, but still on the general subject of sin
in the believer's life, consider the subject of forgiveness.
The Bible contains so many strong and encouraging
promises of divine pardon that it is not difficult to find
texts for comforting and uplifting sermons on Christian
assurance. Yet there are Christians for whom that type of
sermon can act as a very dangerous sort of spiritual ana-
esthetic. These are the *hypo*sensitive or under-sensitive
types; those who by nature have a very high self-image.

They don't worry about a thing. A resilient confidence
exudes from every pore. Like Mr Micawber, they always
look on the bright side of life. No matter what slings and
arrows of outrageous fortune descend upon them, they
always seem to bounce back. Like Norman Vincent Peale,
they think positively about everything, most of all about
themselves.

They have not much patience with fools, scant sympa-
thy with failures and little awareness of the irritation they
cause by their frequently tactless behaviour. They do very
well in job interviews because they have no difficulty at all
in drawing other people's attention to their good points.
And, of course, when they look in the mirror, it is always,
like Narcissus, to admire themselves and preen their
feathers.

A good strong sermon on assurance to these strong-
willed, self-congratulatory types all too easily lulls them
into a gross complacency. 'Ah, yes,' they say, 'what a
wonderful thing to know I have been saved. Sinful acts,
sinful words, sinful thoughts have all been cleansed away.
Sins past, sins present, sins future will never be held
against me. I am filled with the Holy Spirit! I have no
need to fear hell or judgement. I have been lifted out of the
shadow of death, placed in the heavenly realms with
Christ. I don't have to worry about those Ten Commandments any more. Why, to allow yourself to feel guilty is a
lack of faith! What was it Augustine said? "Love God and

do what you like," that's it! Well said, Augustine; you hit the nail on the head. "To the pure all things are pure."'

It was not at all the preacher's intention to encourage a negligent or permissive attitude towards sin, but those who are naturally inclined to belittle their own faults and be optimistic about their own destinies very easily interpret the Christian doctrine of the perseverance of the saints in such a way as to dull their proper sense of moral responsibility. As a result, their consciences are seared and that sermon which was very necessary and true has had the most unfortunate side effects upon them.

The preacher's task, then, is not an enviable one. Whatever he does, he is in danger of misleading someone. He has to comfort the worried and to worry the comfortable: he must preach both and at the same time the necessity of holiness and the security of the believer. In so doing, unless he is very careful, he lays himself wide open to the charge of being self-contradictory and confused. And that is precisely what unsympathetic commentators accuse John of being on this very subject.

Look, for example, at the statement: 'If we claim to be without sin, we deceive ourselves and the truth is not in us' (1:8). Compare that with: 'No one who is born of God will continue to sin, because God's seed remains in him; he cannot go on sinning, because he has been born of God' (3:9). How can two mutually incompatible statements like that be reconciled? Either, say the scholars, the author of 1 John is lacking in intelligence or the whole letter is a hotchpotch of bits and pieces written by different people holding inconsistent views. Yet, what those scholars are neglecting is that John is a preacher and, as every preacher knows, it is a delicate thing to strike a balance on the subject of sin in the life of the Christian.

John was in fact confronting two quite different Christian groups as he wrote. One group, belonging to the hypersensitive, was feeling threatened by the gnostic

heretics' super-spiritual claims. These people were beginning to wonder if they were Christians at all, and they
needed a sermon on assurance to counter their anxious
doubts.

The other group belonged to the hyposensitive camp.
These had embraced gnostic ideas and had grossly in-
flated ideas of their own spiritual prowess as a result.
They needed a strong sermon on holiness to counter their
complacency.

So poor John is caught in the unenviable task of writing
one pastoral letter to meet both these needs simultaneously. It is little wonder that he seems to contradict
himself. Here is the happy hunting ground of Christians
who like proof-texts, because you can prove practically
anything from 1 John if you have a mind to. Arbitrary
quotations from this letter are fatal. There are few books
of the Bible for which it is more important to study the
book as a whole, because John has a balance to strike, and
we can only maintain that balance by holding every statement he makes in tension with every other.

As we go on to look at this subject of sin in the believer's
life from several angles, we shall need to have this in mind
all the time. Indeed, I recommend that you read through
the entire letter at this point, just to make sure that you
are fully informed about everything that John wants to say
on the subject.

The fundamental truth

'This is the message we have heard from him and declare
to you: God is light; in him there is no darkness at all'
(1:5).

There is some dispute among the commentators about
the precise meaning of the word 'light'. It is obviously a
metaphor, for John is not equating God with electro-
magnetic radiation. But the problem is that the figure of

light is used by John and by the Bible generally in two
different ways.

Quite often light is used as a symbol of revelation,
bringing to light things which previously could not be
seen. That meaning would make a certain degree of sense
here, because in verses 1 and 4 John has been speaking
about the light appearing.

But the other way in which light is often used in the
Bible is as a symbol of perfect righteousness. And if you
look at the main context of the passage in which the
statement 'God is light' occurs, I think that is likely to be
the principal thought in John's mind here: light, not as a
symbol of revelation, but rather as one of ethical purity.
When we find him talking in verse 6 about walking in
darkness and in verse 7 about walking in the light, he is
not talking about our vision of God, but about our life
style, our conduct. It is not illumination of the truth that is
the main subject of this passage, but the sanctification of
our lives. In verse 5 the contrast between light and darkness represents not the polarisation between knowledge
and ignorance, but between good and evil.

That being so, it is clear that John is making a statement here about one of the most fundamental questions of
all religious thought: how morality relates to the ultimate
nature of things. Where do good and evil fit in the universe? Are they absolute or are they only artefacts of
man's cultural development? In other words, do we just
label things good and evil or is there a real difference in
kind?

Essentially, there are two different kinds of theory being
held in regard to this question. The first is monism, which
argues that the ultimate reality behind the universe is
unitary, that is singular. Whether it be material, as the
Marxists believe, or spiritual, as say, for example, many
Buddhists believe, everything that happens is a manifestation of one thing. The physicist may call it energy; the

Hindu may call it Brahma; the *Star Wars* enthusiast will call it the Force. But, whatever title you give, good and evil are both part of it. They have to be, by definition, because everything is part of it.

The other theory that prevails historically in answer to this question is dualism, which argues that ultimately the reality behind the universe is binary or twofold. There is one ultimate force of good and one of evil, and they are locked in perpetual antagonism against one another. Sometimes, as in ancient Persian religion, these forces were both reckoned to be spiritual. At other times, as in certain forms of Greek philosophy, the evil part was identified with the material world and the good part with the non-material spirit or reason. Either way, there were two ultimate realities in the universe competing with one another.

The gnostics, whom John has perpetually on his mind as he writes this letter, had their own ideas on the subject. Buffeted as they were by various influences of thought in the Middle East, some monistic and some dualistic, they succeeded in being very confused. Their opinions about it were extremely eccentric and far too complicated for me to go into detail here. Suffice it to say that in some ways they were monistic and in others they were dualistic. They saw God as a kind of spectrum between light and darkness, which started in pure light and went through all shades of grey into pitch blackness, like a television test card. They had a lot in common with the *Star Wars* fanatic. They believed in a Force that had a dark side as well as a good.

'God is light; in him there is no darkness at all' (1:5).

This statement, then, is not to be regarded as just a piece of meaningless rhetoric. John is making a comment about what was then, and in many respects still is today, a most vital controversy.

It is a fascinating statement because, in one sense, it is monistic: there is no doubt that God was singular in

John's mind. God had no rivals. There was no duality of ultimate power in John's universe. This God alone had omnipotence and eternity. John was a good Jew and he knew his creed: 'The Lord our God, the Lord is One.'

Yet, in another sense, this is a dualistic statement, for, against the usual monistic doctrine that good and evil adhere in God, and the gnostic idea that God is morally schizophrenic, John is saying that God is 100% committed to one side of the light/darkness divide. 'God is light', pure and unadulterated, and, as if to reinforce his meaning, he puts it emphatically in the negative also, 'in him there is no darkness at all'. This, he claims, is not just speculation, like the teaching of the philosophers or of the gnostics. It is a revealed truth: '[listen to] the message we have heard from him' (1:5).

This, of course, puts Christianity into a unique category.

The Christian claim is that the God who made this world, in addition to being omnipotent, is totally pure and holy. The question that then arises is where the darkness came from. If it is not a part of God, and is not another eternal force like God, what is its origin and why does God put up with it? The picture of an omnipotent God who for some crazy reason allows evil to enter his universe and to continue there seems extraordinary. Yet the frustrating thing is that neither John nor anybody else in the Bible ever answers that question. The darkness is there. We are told it has no part in the light. We are told it can never triumph over the light because God is light, but how it came to be there in the first place and why it is permitted to continue for one second in God's universe we are never clearly told.

Augustine speculated that because the darkness is essentially negative, it does not need to be created. It is simply the negation of all the positive qualities that God is. You may find that argument convincing or you may not.

But the Bible never explicitly says such a thing. All we are at liberty to say is what John says, that God is light. There is no dark side to this force, not even a gnostic twilight zone. He is all light and nothing but light. His righteousness is perfect; it is peerless, unadulterated. This, says John, is the fundamental truth of God's character which is revealed in God's word. At the same time it constitutes the root of man's deepest problem. For if God is light, then by nature he is a destroyer of darkness, and, wherever that darkness came from, one thing is sure, there is plenty of it in us.

Three false responses

How do we respond to the fact that God is light? What answer do we find to the darkness of our own souls? The gnostics had some answers, but unfortunately they were all simplistic—easy, cheap, and inadequate.

'The darkness makes no difference to me'

'We claim to have fellowship with him yet walk in the darkness,' (1:6) they said.

In other words: 'I can sin with impunity. Moral failure does not affect my experience of God. I have fellowship with God even though my life style is corrupt.' That, alas, is not such an uncommon claim. Many of the varieties of spiritual experience which this world knows have no ethical components at all.

Yoga, for instance, is in a religious sense a way of experiencing God, at least as the Hindu understands God, but most forms of Yoga have no moral component. It is just a mystical technique, which is precisely what the gnostics were concerned with. Some of them were saying,

> Oh, sleeping with your neighbour's wife won't hinder your
> contact with God, any more than it can stop your tran-
> scendental meditation. How can deeds done in the body
> affect what goes on in the spirit? The two worlds are
> completely separate.

Tragically, this same kind of amoral spirituality has at
times been advocated in the Christian church. Tech-
nically, it was called antinomianism and, whilst it is historically a rather complicated subject about which it is not
easy to generalise, it is fair to say that, at worst, the
antinomians argued precisely what verse 6 says, that a
man's relationship with God is in no way affected by the
moral quality of his life. We can sin with impunity.

John has a short answer to that. If we say that, he says,
'we lie and do not live by the truth'. It is a deliberate
falsehood. If we experience a spirituality which is not
morally sensitive, then it is not Christian spirituality we
are experiencing. Maybe that experience derives from our
own human psyche, or maybe it is demonic in origin, but
it does not derive from the spirit of Jesus, for he is the *Holy*
Spirit. Nobody who really knows what it is to have fellowship with God could ever deny the importance of sin or
pretend that sin does not affect his relationship with God.

'The darkness has no part in me'

The second inadequate response is: 'We claim to be without sin' (1:8).

In other words, 'I am essentially good. Any tinge of
darkness in my life is a contamination from the outside; it
does not derive from the inner kernel of my spirit. In my
heart I have no sin.'

Again this is not an uncommon claim. The best example of this kind of moral optimism in recent years is the
humanist movement. Humanists claim, as did the gnostics, that sin is all external, a contamination of the outside

of man due to his behavioural conditioning or animal origins. We do not have to worry about it, as education and evolution will eliminate it all in due time. Evil is not an intractable problem: man can solve it; man is solving it; man is essentially good.

John's answer is again blunt and uncompromising: 'If we claim to be without sin, we deceive ourselves and the truth is not in us' (1:8).

It is all self-delusion and I suppose one of the few hopeful things about the generation in which we live, is that that delusion is beginning to become evident. Shut your eyes to Hitler's gas chambers, Stalin's purges and the crushed skulls of Cambodia and you may convince yourself that there is no essential evil in man! But in our twentieth century, it is becoming painfully obvious just how brutal and selfish man is by nature; he always has been and always will be. It is delusion all right. We deceive ourselves if we say we have no sin, for we certainly deceive nobody else.

'The darkness can be fully overcome by me'

'We claim we have not sinned' (1:10).

In other words, 'I can live a perfect life. Oh yes, sin is a serious matter, I don't dispute that, John. Yes, the human nature is impregnated with sin, but I can rise above my fallen nature. I can triumph over its desires. I can have the testimony "I have not sinned." I can live a perfect life.'

It is possible that the gnostics claimed this to be one of the benefits of their mystical experiences. But it is very far from being unknown in Christian circles, even in recent history. It is essentially the claim of Perfectionism, the Wesleyan holiness movement which had a very influential impact on the Keswick Convention in its earlier years. Perfectionists claim that there is a holiness, which once grasped and appropriated, guarantees a sinless life. They talk about a second experience of the Holy Spirit which makes a person, not just forgiven, but holy. They can even give you a date and time when they became sanctified.

Once again, John is hardly ambiguous about that kind of claim: 'If we claim we have not sinned, we make him out to be a liar and his word has no place in our lives' (1:10).

For John this is the most preposterous error of all. To claim to be perfect is not just a deliberate lie or a sad, self-delusion. The man making such a claim is insulting God. He is directly contradicting the revealed truth of God, and that implies that God is himself deceitful.

Spurgeon was once confronted by a perfectionist, who told him that he had discovered the secret of sinless perfection. Whereupon, we are told, Spurgeon trod heavily on his foot, and his sinless perfection dissolved!

In each of these false replies the realities of Christian experience are not faced up to. They are all pathetically inadequate responses to the problem of how a human being who lives in the darkness can possibly have a personal relationship with a God who lives in unapproachable light. Perfectionism, humanism or antinomianism: none of them will do.

The Christian remedy

John urges us not to despair because there is an answer which, unlike these trite and naïve solutions, works. Unlike the antinomian's, the real answer to this problem treats the importance of sin seriously. Unlike the humanist's, it treats the existence of sin honestly. Unlike the perfectionist's, it treats the power of sin realistically. That answer is the Christian remedy.

> My dear children, I write this to you so that you will not sin. But if anybody does sin, we have one who speaks to

the Father in our defence—Jesus Christ, the Righteous
One. He is the atoning sacrifice for our sins, and not only
for ours but also for the sins of the whole world (2:1,2).

Here the pastoral heart of John displays itself at its
clearest. Notice the fatherly tone, 'My dear children'. He
is concerned for these people. This is not just a theological
treatise on sin. It is a sermon and, as we said at the
beginning of this chapter, it has two aims. On the one
hand, it aims to warn the complacent of the dangers of
their permissive attitudes. On the other hand, it aims to
console the conscience-stricken with the assurance of
God's provision of forgiveness. So he says, 'I write this to
you so that you will not sin.' That is one aim, 'But if
anybody does sin....' Do you see the tension there? What
John has to offer is neither an excuse for sin nor a counsel
of perfection, but a remedy designed by God to meet the
real needs of sinners like us in a fallen world.

Commitment to God's standards

John tells us three things are involved if we are truly to
come to know God in this distinctive Christian way.

First of all, our lives must be committed to God's standards. 'If we walk in the light, as he is in the light, we have
fellowship with one another, and the blood of Jesus, his
Son, purifies us from all sin' (1:7).

When John says, 'If we walk in the light,' he cannot be
saying that perfection is possible, for clearly in verse 10 he
contradicts it. No, the Christian must accept the inev-
itability of failure, as Paul does in Romans chapter 7:

> I know that nothing good lives in me, that is, in my sinful
> nature. For I have the desire to do what is good, but I
> cannot carry it out. For what I do is not the good I want to
> do; no, the evil I do not want to do—this I keep on doing
> (Rom 7:18,19).

What John does mean by 'walk in the light' is living a life which is conscientiously ordered by God's revealed nature. It means, if you like, the end of our moral rebellion; the end of our deliberate deeds that contravene God's law and contradict his character. For a Christian, renewed by the Holy Spirit, that is possible, even though perfection is not. It is important to note that when John says in chapter 2, verse 1, 'if anybody does sin', the tense that he uses in the Greek implies isolated acts of sin as opposed to a general and habitual practice of sin.

John is not as inconsistent in his ideas of sin in the life of the believer as some people make out. He believes that the Christian life should be different. Indeed, if it is not different, something has gone wrong, for if we walk in the darkness, we lie about our fellowship with God. But he does not believe in perfectionism. It is inevitable that isolated acts of sin will continue to infect our lives, even though Christ has redirected their general tenor.

We must expect sin in the life of the believer in that sense. That is normal Christian experience and must not cast us into despair. It does not mean that we are not walking in the light. What is commanded of us here is a transition from a stance of moral rebellion against God's standards to a stance of moral obedience towards those standards. In a word it is conversion.

Paul says, conversion is being transferred from the kingdom of darkness into the kingdom of light, and when we make that transfer, we start to live differently. We know conversion has happened, by the moral change it produces. A Christian's life, then, is committed to God's standards. Even though sometimes he fails to keep them, he tries to keep them; he wants to keep them and is disappointed when he does not. His whole life's progress is a constant attempt in the power of God to live more in the light of those standards.

Some people think that you become a Christian just by making a verbal profession. 'Right, hands up, I'm a Christian now.' That is not enough. Others think that becoming a Christian is just a matter of 'having the warm fuzzies', a big emotional orgy of sentimentality in a church service. But such an experience is not enough, either. Still others think that becoming a Christian is just giving mental assent to a series of propositions: 'Yes, Jesus is God. Yes, Jesus died for our sins. Yes, Jesus is coming again. Yes, I've got all those ticked.' But such a creed is not enough either.

The gnostics made big claims. They had experiences. And the very word 'gnostic' means 'I know', so knowledge was no problem to them. Yet, it is not what we say, what we feel or what we know that makes us a Christian. The primary root of becoming a Christian is obedience. The truth is something that must be done in our lives.

If you are hesitant about how to become a Christian, start practising the Christian life style. You will not do it perfectly, you are not required to do it perfectly, but, says John, there must be a sincere intention of obedience: a life committed to God's standards.

Being open to God's gaze

'If we confess our sins, he is faithful and just and will forgive us our sins and purify us from all unrighteousness' (1:9).

You must have heard the little rhyme about the Garden of Eden:

> Adam blamed Eve,
> Eve blamed the serpent
> And the serpent hadn't got a leg to stand on.

How typically human that is! We always want to pass the buck: 'It's not my fault; he's to blame.' I think maybe that is why the Bible never reveals the answer to the problem of the origin of evil. It is not that there is no answer to the problem, but that man's interest in finding the answer is an unworthy one. We only really want to know the origin of evil because we are looking for an excuse. We want to say, 'There, that's why I did it. It was my genetics, wasn't it?' 'It's my social background.' 'It's my sex drive.' 'It was the capitalist system.' 'It was the Devil. He's the one to blame!'

So man wants to rationalise his sin in order to evade its guilt, but the Bible won't allow us to do that. Evil cannot be explained. There is never a valid reason for our sin. According to the Bible, sin, by definition, is an act of culpable folly. There may have been mitigating circumstances, or others implicated in our crime, but all that does is moderate the penalty, it does not reverse the verdict. We are guilty, and the only valid response to sin, therefore, is confession: 'I did it. The sin began in me.' We are not permitted to look for some origin of sin behind men. We are responsible for it. We brought it into the world.

Yet confession is humiliating. Man prefers to keep his self-respect by looking for excuses. John says that if we would have fellowship with God, we must accept responsibility for our actions. The buck stops here. Confess.

This means that if the first requirement to become a Christian is obedience, a sincere intention to do God's will in our lives, then the second requirement to enter on authentic Christian experience is prayer, confessional prayer. We must talk to God about our sin, not because he does not know about it, but because only by facing up to the offence we have caused him and saying 'sorry' can there ever possibly be a relationship of normality between us again.

There is a story told in Africa of a servant who stole his master's chicken. He thought he had got away with it but then the next day one of his work-mates came up and said, 'I saw you steal that chicken,' and started to blackmail him. From that day on his life was riddled with problems.

He had the problem of finding the money to pay off his blackmailer and there was tension between him and his master.

'It is no good,' he said, 'I shall have to do something about it. I shall have to make a clean breast of it.' So he went to the master and said, 'You know that chicken you lost the other week, I stole it.'

'I know you did,' said the master.

'You know?'

'Oh, yes,' said the master, 'I saw you do it. I have been waiting all this time for you to come and tell me.'

The irony of our sin is that we cannot tell God anything about ourselves that he does not already know. He knows the very worst about us, but there can never be a relationship between us till we are happy that he knows and so are willing to talk to him about it. That is why prayer must come right at the beginning of Christian experience. We must open our lives to the gaze of God, whose eyes we cannot evade anyway.

John says that if we fulfil these two conditions, we can be sure that our lives are immune from his judgement. And he tells us that three times:

> If we walk in the light...the blood of Jesus, his Son, purifies us from all sin (1:7).
>
> If we confess our sins, he is faithful and just and will forgive us our sins and purify us from all unrighteousness (1:9).
>
> If anybody does sin, we have one who speaks to the Father in our defence—Jesus Christ, the Righteous One. He is the atoning sacrifice for our sins, and not only for ours but also for the sins of the whole world (2:1,2).

When our case comes up before the highest court in the universe, if we are Christians, we can be absolutely sure of acquittal because we have the best lawyer in the universe: Jesus Christ, the righteous, speaks to the Father on our behalf. More important in a sense even than that, we have the best defence in the universe. It is not that our lawyer will bid us plead innocent; he is not a liar. Nor can we plead mitigating circumstances, for that won't change the verdict. No, his plea for us is unanswerable! It is that the penalty has already been paid. The sentence has already been discharged. That is what the expression 'atoning sacrifice for our sins' means. Jesus on the cross was taking our place, paying our price, fulfilling our sentence.

Chapter 3

The World
1 John 2:3–17

Knowing God

If I were to tell you I was personally acquainted with the Queen, I suppose you would be impressed or perhaps a little sceptical. But for someone to say, 'I know God,' is surely either arrogance or lunacy. Yet that is the claim we as Christians make. Eternal life was defined by Jesus in precisely those terms: 'Now this is eternal life: that they may know you, the only true God, and Jesus Christ, whom you have sent' (John 17:3). But how can anybody be sure that the knowledge of God is actually theirs? That was an issue of great importance to the church to which John was writing this first letter.

One of the characteristics of the gnostic false teachers who were troubling the church was that they talked very persuasively and very eloquently about knowing God. This is in fact how they got their name, from the Greek, *gnosis*, meaning knowledge. Whereas an agnostic is a person who does not know whether there is a God or not, the gnostics by contrast said very emphatically that they did know.

The trouble was that the kind of knowledge of God about which these false teachers boasted was different from the one which the apostles taught. As a result, the Christians in Asia to whom John was writing were getting thoroughly confused. 'How are we to tell who knows God and who doesn't?' they were asking themselves. More important still: 'How are we to be sure whether we ourselves know God or not? For clearly somebody is being deceived. Maybe it is us.'

John's major purpose in writing this letter is to reassure these perplexed, but orthodox Christians. One of the main ways he does this is by defining certain criteria which distinguish a person who really knows God from an impostor. It constitutes an interesting parallel to the Gospel that also bears John's name, because the Gospel, we are told, was written to non-Christians in order to persuade and encourage them to embrace Christianity. John writes very near the end of his Gospel: 'These are written that you may believe that Jesus is the Christ, the Son of God, and that by believing you may have life in his name' (Jn 20:31). Accordingly, the Gospel is characterised by signs, designed to awaken saving faith in those who as yet did not have it.

This letter, on the other hand, is written to Christians, not to persuade them to believe, but to reassure them that they have truly embraced Christ, and so, at the end of this letter, we read: 'I write these things to you who believe in the name of the Son of God so that you may know that you have eternal life' (5:13). Accordingly, this letter is not characterised by signs designed to produce faith, but by tests designed to accredit it.

These fall into two broad categories: tests of Christian life style and those of Christian doctrine. They correspond to what John describes as being the two great enemies of spiritual life and, therefore, of Christian assurance. In this chapter we will consider the world's attack on our life style.

The test of Christian obedience

'We know that we have come to know him if we obey his commands' (2:3).

Part of the trouble about the phrase 'knowing God' is that we use the verb 'to know' in different ways. There is a whole branch of philosophy called epistemology, which deals with working out what exactly we mean by knowing something. Think, for example, of these two statements:

> I know that the grass is green.
> I know that fear is dreadful.

The first proposition is about an object external to myself, grass, and the observation I am making about it derives from the physical senses; it is green. That is conventionally called objective knowledge.

The second proposition, however, is about an emotion internal to myself, fear, and the observation I am making about it is a value judgement in which the physical senses play little part; it is dreadful. That is conventionally called subjective knowledge.

Over the centuries, philosophers have oscillated in regard to the weight they give to these two kinds of knowledge. In the eighteenth and nineteenth centuries, empiricists emphasised objective knowledge. This was said to be reliable because it could be verified with scientific methods. You can take the grass into your laboratory and establish without any doubt that it is green.

In this century there has been a swing back towards subjectivism in the philosophy of the existentialists. They emphasise subjective knowledge obtained through emotions, which form the essential core of our human experience. Even people who have no awareness of this philosophical debate, who never read erudite books with such words as 'empiricism' and 'existentialism' in them, tend to lean in one direction or other in this debate. Some tend to be objective and others subjective; some are hard-headed rationalists, while others are soft-hearted senti-mentalists.

It is often said that this division in attitude is sex linked: that men prefer their masculine logic, while ladies like their feminine intuition. Whatever the truth of that is, suffice it to say that when we use the phrase 'I know', it can introduce statements both of objective fact and of subjective feeling.

It is important that we appreciate that the gnostics were subjectivists. When they talked about knowing God, they were not referring to concrete facts that one could verbalise, but rather about mystical experience. God for them belonged to the realm of feelings.

I suspect they had a great deal in common with the Hindu sects that were very popular in the 1970s. One of them had a guru who used to have a big photograph of himself on their advertisements and underneath was the invitation: 'Let me introduce you to God.' What he was actually offering was a technique of meditation, which if pursued with sufficient determination, produced psyche-delic hallucinations and emotional disturbances in the subject, which were interpreted by the guru as experienc-ing the divine. Interestingly, those who were initiated into this particular Eastern cult were said to have 'taken the guru's knowledge'. In all probability the gnostics, influ-enced as they were by Eastern ideas, were offering some-thing very similar in the field of religious experience: that was what their *gnosis* amounted to.

It is particularly interesting to note how John responds to that challenge. Here is a group of so-called Christians who are highly subjectivist, who want to reduce Christian experience to something totally in the realm of the emo-tions. They want to make it something mystical, unrelated to concrete facts, to history, or even to the physical world. Yet he does not do what perhaps some of us would be inclined to do, and deny that there is an experiential element in Christianity. Nor does he say that mysticism has nothing to do with Christianity, because that would not be true either. Indeed, John, of all the New Testament writers, is the most mystical.

Instead, he introduces a parameter into this whole debate about knowing God which was conspicuous by its absence from the gnostics' speculations. In verse 3 he introduces the subject of ethics. However you interpret 'to know him', 'We know that we have come to know him if we obey his commands' (2:3). He takes Christian assurance out of the realm of esoteric experience, whether or not it is valid, and places it instead in the concrete, observable, objective world of moral conduct.

Significantly, he puts it there because to him, the God of Christian revelation is a moral God. Nobody who has understood Jesus could have any doubt about that, as he has made clear in the opening verses of the chapter. It is obvious that God is a moral God first of all because of the person Jesus was. He was, according to verse 1, 'the Righteous One'. Everything about Jesus was morally good.

It is evident, secondly, that the God of Christian revelation is indeed a moral God because of the work Jesus came to do. 'He is the atoning sacrifice for our sins' (2:2). The whole purpose of his coming was not to impart some esoteric experience, but to deal with the problem of judgement on our sinful lives.

Thirdly, it is clear because of the role which Jesus now fulfils on our behalf in heaven. 'If anybody does sin, we have one who speaks to the Father in our defence—Jesus Christ' (2:1). He is now in heaven not to impart strange experiences to us, but to make sure that, whenever any sin occurs in our lives, God remembers that we belong to him and that Jesus' blood was shed for us. From first to last, Jesus witnesses to a God who is passionately concerned about sin.

According to John, if that is so, the first test by which to evaluate whether those who claim to know God really do so is to enquire whether they share this passionate moral concern: 'The man who says, "I know him", but does not do what he commands is a liar, and the truth is not in him' (2:4). He takes assurance out of the realm of subjective experience, which we can all debate, and places it on the objective rock of Christian conduct. Notice how this moral sensitivity should declare itself, according to John: by obeying his commands or, in other words, by paying attention to the rules. That is significant because there has been a movement in recent years, very much in line with the general subjectivist inclination of our century, to play down rules as a guide to Christian action and to choose instead a more mystical approach. You will often find people quoting, 'If you are led by the Spirit, you are not under law' (Gal 5:18), which they interpret to mean that Christian morality is not a matter of obedience to a moral code, but of being directed by some mysterious inner impulses.

I am sure that John has no intention of denying the role of the Holy Spirit in guiding our lives, but it is clear he believes that rules still exist for Christians. There are certain things that Christians do and there are certain things Christians do not do, and their obedience to these moral absolutes provides an objective test of their relationship with God. One of the arguments which is often used for doing away with rules is that they are inconsistent with love. For example, Joseph Fletcher in his book, *Situation Ethics*, suggests there that rules destroy the spontaneity of love. He says that love, like a built-in moral compass needle, automatically homes in on the right course of action. Sometimes it will fit the rule and sometimes it will not, because love is flexible enough to respond to each new situation on its merits.[2]

Yet John does not see rules as contradictory to love: 'If anyone obeys his word, God's love is truly made complete in him. This is how we know we are in him: Whoever claims to live in him must walk as Jesus did' (2:5,6). The way of love is not to surrender to mystical promptings or spiritual hunches or sentimental feelings, he says. The way of love is to study God's word, to study Christ's example and then to seek conscientiously to model our lives on these objective guidelines. The man who does that is one in whom God's love is made perfect, or complete. Love does not abolish God's rules, it obeys them.

In fact Jesus said as much: 'If you love me, you will obey what I command' (Jn 14:15). The first way in which the world seeks to undermine our assurance is by undermining our obedience. The first test that we really know God is that of obedience.

The test of Christian affections

'Anyone who claims to be in the light but hates his brother is still in the darkness. Whoever loves his brother lives in the light' (2:9,10).

In this letter John's thoughts tend to move in circles. He has a fairly small number of themes, but instead of dealing with them in sequence, he circles round them, trying to demonstrate by the very spiral structure of his letter the complex relationship that exists between various aspects of God's truth. Love, which is a constantly recurring theme, is mentioned here briefly, but dealt with more extensively in chapter 3 and then at even greater length in chapter 4. (So, rather than go into great detail on the subject at this point, I shall focus on it in a later chapter.)

What we do need to note here is John's teaching that love, Christian affection for our fellow Christians, is a second and vital test of authentic Christian experience, and for that he gives us three reasons.

Love is the primary commandment

The first reason he gives is that love is the primary commandment: 'I am not writing you a new command but an old one, which you have had since the beginning' (2:7). Almost certainly, the reference here is to where Jesus says: 'A new command I give you: Love one another' (Jn 13:34).

What I have to say to you about love, then, belongs to that corpus of apostolic teaching upon which the church's life had been built from its very earliest days.

Unlike the gnostics, John had no theological novelty to offer. As an orthodox Christian, John can only remind his readers of what in fact they already ought to know, the old commandment, the message they had already heard. It must be so.

Love is the sign of the new age

At the same time, John says that there is a sense in which this commandment is new, because it is the sign of the new age. And that is the second reason why love must be part of our Christian lives. 'Yet I am writing you a new command; its truth is seen in him and you, because the darkness is passing and the true light is already shining' (2:8).

It was John's firm conviction that something had happened in Jesus which had driven a wedge into history. We call the years BC and AD, and rightly so, because there is, as it were, a discontinuity in the graph of history occurring right there in Jesus.

As long ago as Moses, men had realised that the key to a happy world was that man should love his neighbour, but unfortunately the darkness of sin prevented such a paradisiacal society from ever materialising, as it still frustrates the would-be Utopias of today. But, says John, something has happened in Jesus that makes it all different, for in Jesus the age of darkness has ended and the new age of God's light has begun. Jesus is the signal of the dawning of a new world, that of love. And the church is the signpost to that new world.

That is what John means when he says, 'Its truth is seen in him and you.' The commandment to love has at last become a practical possibility, something men can not only dream about, but actually see. It is no longer an unattainable ideal, but a glorious possibility in the community of God's people. So, if we truly know God, if we are part of this new age that Jesus has wrought, by definition, love will be there.

Its absence invites error

Thirdly, John says love must be present in authentic Christian experience, because its absence is an invitation to error.

> Whoever loves his brother lives in the light, and there is nothing in him to make him stumble. But whoever hates his brother is in the darkness and walks around in the darkness; he does not know where he is going, because the darkness has blinded him (2:10,11).

One of the less attractive things about the gnostics was their contempt for people who did not share their super-spiritual ideas. They were an élitist group, who drew a distinction in the church between the ignorant masses and themselves, the enlightened spiritual aristocrats. Later on, in chapter 2, verse 19, there is even a suggestion that some of them had recently hived off into a clique on their own: 'They went out from us, but they did not really belong to us.' No doubt the main congregation was not spiritual enough for them, so they decided to go it alone.

In some ways, as far as John is concerned, this was the most damning thing about these false teachers, because people who despise their Christian brothers and sisters in this supercilious way, give away the fact that, whatever

claims they make to spirituality, they are grossly mal-
adjusted in their spiritual vision. They walk in the darkness; they are in error; people who do not love one another
inevitably make mistakes in the spiritual realm. Authentic
Christianity is marked out by love for all Christian people,
whatever their party label.

In all likelihood, that is the reason for the rather strange
interlude that follows in verses 12 to 14. The repetition of
'children', 'fathers' and 'young men' borders on the
poetic, and commentators puzzle about who are being
designated by these three titles. What distinction is John
drawing here? Is it based on age, on church office, or on
spiritual maturity?

I suggest that John would answer that it is based on all
three. He enjoys being enigmatic and ambiguity is nearly
always intentional with him. I think what he is trying to
say here is: 'Look, I am writing to anybody and everybody
in the church. My letter is for all of you, wherever you see
yourself, whether you are young or old, experienced or
inexperienced, weak or strong, holding office or just a lay
member of the congregation. Unlike the gnostics, I love
you all. Whatever your level of Christian experience,
whatever the nature of your Christian experience, I am
concerned for you all. I recognise no hierarchy of spiritual
grace. I affirm you all as my brothers and sisters in Christ.
You are all my children, my friends. This is the kind of
love that marks out those who truly have fellowship with
God, as opposed to these super-spiritual types who hive
off on their own because you are not good enough for
them.'

John sees love and loyalty to the orthodox Christian
group as essential if we are really to be sure that we are
Christians. If the world cannot stop us obeying, it will try
to stop us loving. And if it is unable to stop us loving, it
will try to make us love the wrong thing.

The test of Christian values

'Do not love the world or anything in the world. If anyone
loves the world, the love of the Father is not in him' (2:15).

There are few things more widely misinterpreted or
misunderstood than worldliness. What does John mean
by not loving the world?

Not pharisaism

In the first place there are certain things we can say with
absolute assurance John definitely does not mean when he
tells us not to love the world. He is not talking about
pharisaism, for instance. The Pharisees, that Jesus had so
many encounters with, were very concerned to be non-
worldly. Surrounded as they were by a pagan culture,
which threatened their Judaism, they wanted very much
to be different from the world, but the way they went
about it was condemned by Jesus.

They tried to be distinct from the world by having
endless rules about what one could and could not do on
the Sabbath. They discriminated about the company they
kept: it was worldly to mix with sinful, disreputable,
undesirable people. Furthermore, they had all sorts of
regulations about what one could eat and drink, and how
one did it.

Ironically, these three aspects of pharisaism are in precisely the areas of life style which many, many Christians
think important. If one is not a worldly Christian, one
does not wash one's car on Sunday: one keeps the Sabbath. If one is not a worldly Christian, one does not go to
the wrong sort of parties, nor does one consume alcohol.
Many Christians identify worldliness with exactly the
same sort of things as did the Pharisees.

But Jesus got into trouble with the Pharisees because he
broke all their petty regulations in this regard. He did not
keep the Sabbath in the approved way. He scandalised

them by keeping company with sinners and he did not have a great deal of time for their restrictions on food and drink. So, whatever loving the world means, it is not a matter of these kinds of pharisaical rules, by which the Pharisees, and still some Christians today, tried to define worldliness.

Not asceticism

Denying the world is not asceticism either. Very early in the life of the early church the idea gained acceptance that the more you denied the flesh, the less worldly you were. Many of the early church Fathers practised such ascetic disciplines as celibacy. The Syrian church at one stage went so far as to state that you could not become a church member if you were married.

Fasting was advocated not just to give oneself opportunity for single-minded prayer, but with the idea that the more one's body was emaciated, the more God was inclined to listen to one. They renounced worldly goods and went around in rags; they never washed; they let their hair grow; and sometimes, even more directly masochistic disciplines like flagellation were involved.

Whatever virtues the simple life style may have, this kind of ascetic extremism has nothing whatsoever to do with worldliness as the New Testament understands it because it denies the doctrine of creation. The Bible tells us that God made the world and he made it good. The Bible never submits to that kind of Greek dualism that wants to say that the material world is all bad and only the spiritual things are good. The world, as created by God, is good and for that reason Paul in 1 Timothy 4:4 bids us combat asceticism. People who deny marriage or deny that one should eat certain foods, he says, are preaching a doctrine of demons. For everything created is to be accepted with thanksgiving by the Christian. So

whatever 'do not love the world' means, it does not mean
that we should practise asceticism.

There is a third thing, too, that John does not mean. By
'do not love the world', he is not advocating monasticism,
withdrawing into a holy huddle. John Stott calls this
'being rabbit-hole Christians'. He has in mind the Christian student, for example, who pops his head out of his
burrow (which he shares with a Christian room-mate) in
the morning and runs along to his classroom, where he sits
with his Christian class-mates. After class he proceeds to
lunch, where he frantically searches for the table where all
his Christian friends are eating. When evening comes, he
goes back to his Bible study, attended just by Christians,
where he prays fervently for all the non-believers at his
college. Then he scurries back to his Christian room-mate,
safe again. So he has spent all day dashing furiously from
one Christian burrow to another—a 'rabbit-hole Christian'!

That is far removed from what John means by not
loving the world. He is not talking here about living in
monastic isolation from non-Christian society. That will
not do for a very simple reason: we have to evangelise the
world. Did Jesus sit in the synagogue with a big notice
outside saying: 'The gospel will be preached in this synagogue next Sabbath—everybody welcome'? No, rather
he went into the world to the prostitutes of Samaria, to tax
collectors and fishermen about their daily work, to the sick
in their need, to housewives in their homes, to the crowds
in the city, to the intellectuals in the corridors of learning.
So often we have adopted a ghetto mentality, shrinking
back into the safety of our Bible study groups and our
church services for fear of that big, bad world that might
contaminate us.

Let us not forget that this world, which John says it is
perilous for us to love, is the same world which God so
loved that he gave his Son to die for it. 'Do not love the

world' cannot possibly mean withdraw contact from the world. Jesus said, as he prayed for his disciples: 'As you sent me into the world, I have sent them into the world' (Jn 17:18).

So what does 'do not love the world' mean in practice? John spells it out for us: 'For everything in the world—the cravings of sinful man, the lust of his eyes and the boasting of what he has and does—comes not from the Father but from the world' (2:16).

'The cravings of sinful man'

There are certain things in this world that God did not put there. Much of what is here in the world God put there by creation, but the something else which he did not put there is sin. It is that bit of the world which is not from the Father and which is so often characteristic of the world in general, that we must not love.

'The cravings of sinful man', as the NIV renders it, is a better translation than the AV's, 'the lusts of the flesh', because almost inevitably that has sexual connotations for us today and while John's phrase includes sensuality, it is broader than that. He is probably talking about every desire that arises from our physical appetites: gluttony, greed, addiction and so on. This is the kind of worldliness that indulges the body, and which he urges us not to love.

'The lust of his eyes'

By 'the lust of the eyes', John means a covetousness that arises from the desire for aesthetic rather than physical satisfaction. It is important to realise that lust is not the monopoly of the pornography business. It is true that some men will sell their souls to possess a woman's body, but it is also true that some men will sell their souls to possess a great painting, or even a rare postage stamp. This is the worldliness which indulges its whims and fancies extravagantly and it is no less intemperate or unspiritual than the lust of the flesh.

'The boasting of what he has and does'

The Greek phrase has the flavour of the braggart who is for ever proclaiming how much this or that possession in his household cost, or how wonderful that expensive luxury cruise in the Mediterranean was. If John were alive today, he would probably use the phrase, 'status symbols'. 'The boasting of what he has and does' is the worldliness that indulges our pride.

Worldliness that indulges our bodies, worldliness that indulges our whims and fancies, or our pride, that is what it means to love the world. It is the man who looks at the prostitute in the street and says, 'I must have it; I need it; it's natural.' It is the woman who looks at the diamond necklace in the jeweller's window: 'I must have it. I can't resist it, it's beautiful.' It is the worldliness of the young couple looking at the smart new modern house on the new estate. 'We must have it, we can't do without it. We have got to keep up with the Joneses.'

That is the love of the world that John is talking about. It means to give the world your heart, to put it at the centre of your affections, to make of the world what Jesus calls your treasure. As John makes clear, people who do that give themselves away. No matter how religious they may seem, no matter what extravagant claims of spirituality they may make, if they love the world, the love of the Father is not in them because 'the world and its desires pass away, but the man who does the will of God lives for ever' (2:7).

There is a law of corruption in the universe: things disintegrate spontaneously. The car you buy this year will be rusty in five years and in ten years it will be an absolute wreck. The pyramids of Egypt are Pharaohs' attempts at immortality. Yet time from those pyramids is making dust. You may lock up all your gold and silver in a big chest but still, even if nothing else does, death will steal it from you.

> Our life is but an empty show,
> Naked we come and naked go,
> Both for the humble and the proud,
> There are no pockets in a shroud.[3]

What John says is right. The world and its desires pass away. It is temporary. Materialism is a stupid philosophy: it means investing everything in what will one day become nothing. Love is intended for people not for the world, because people last and things do not. If we want to invest in eternity, we must learn to love people, not the world with its extravagant materialism, its crude sensualism and its prestigious exhibitionism.

It is the mark of the Christian that he has learnt that lesson, that his life is focused upon personal values. And it shows: in his ambitions; in the way he furnishes his home; in the books on his bookshelf and in the way he spends his money.

Chapter 4

The Lie

1 John 2:18–27; 4:1–6

In 1823 a man called Smith claimed he received a visitation from an angel called Moroni, who directed him to some gold plates hidden on a hill near Palmyra in New York State. According to Smith, the plates were inscribed with ancient Egyptian hieroglyphics, which he was enabled miraculously to translate by means of a specially provided pair of angelic spectacles. The translation revealed extraordinary facts about the early history of the American continent, not least that America was not discovered by Christopher Colombus, as you and I were taught, but by a Jewish prophet called Lehi, 600 years before Christ, and that Christ himself appeared after his resurrection to the descendants of that ancient Jewish family in the New World.

I find all that incredible, but three million adherents of the Church of the Latter Day Saints, popularly known as the Mormons, believe it all.

The greatest problem for the Christian church today is not so much the rise of scientific scepticism in the last hundred years or so, as the growth of public gullibility. As Chesterton said, 'When people abandon the truth, they don't believe in nothing, they believe in anything.' There are thousands of cults and sects in our world today, many of them one would have thought straining the credulity of Simple Simon by their bizarre and fantastic speculations. Yet all of them by their numerical success prove the accuracy of Chesterton's assertion.

The church does not have to worry about atheism. That ephemeral superstition has never seriously threatened the essential religious consciousness of mankind. The success that Marxism claims in propagating it behind the Iron Curtain has only been achieved by such vicious policies of repression as incarcerating Christian pastors in Siberia, or incinerating Moslem tribesmen in Afghanistan. No, the real danger is not unbelief, but wrong belief; not irreligion, but heresy; not the doubter, but the deceiver.

It is so in our day in the latter part of the twentieth century and the passage that we study in this chapter indicates that it was also so in John's day, in the latter part of the first century.

We have already seen that one of the major purposes John has in writing this first letter is to define certain criteria by which the authenticity of a person's Christian profession can be tested. These tests fall into two broad categories, and we now look at the second of these, tests of doctrine and the enemy of Christian assurance that corresponds to it—the lie.

'Dear children, this is the last hour; and as you have heard that the Antichrist is coming, even now many antichrists have come. This is how we know it is the last hour' (2:18).

One of the most fundamental things about Christians is that they are people who live looking forward to the end of the world. This is certainly not true for most people, who run away from the mere thought of it, but Christians are odd in this respect. They live with the end of the world on their minds all the time, or at least they should.

Jesus emphatically warned the disciples before he left this world that he would come again, not this time as an insignificant peasant of Galilee, but as the Son of Man 'in clouds with great power and glory' (Mk 13:26). No one would have advance notice of his arrival, it would be sudden and unexpected, but in the interval between his departure and his return, a number of things would happen, the so-called signs of the last time. Believers who were vigilant, when they observed these diagnostic events, would be reassured that it was indeed the eleventh hour and that history was on course, moving swiftly to its culmination in Jesus' return.

It is against this backdrop of Jesus' teaching that we have to understand what John is saying here, for one of the signs of the end that Jesus talked about was the rise of religious imposters. Jesus warned that false Christs and false prophets would appear: 'Many will come in my name, claiming, "I am the Christ," and will deceive many' (Mt 24:5), and this sombre expectation of traitors infiltrating the Christian community remained a fixed part of the teaching of the apostles right through the formative years of the church. 'I know,' said Paul, to the elders at Ephesus, '...after I leave, savage wolves will come in among you and will not spare the flock. Even from your own number men will arise and distort the truth in order to draw away disciples after them' (Acts 20:29,30). There are similar statements from all the apostles.

What is interesting about these verses in 1 John, though, is that they link together this anticipated apostasy in the church with another sign of the end which seems in the earlier teaching of Jesus and the apostles to be distinct from it. That is the figure of the Antichrist.

The Antichrist

The prefix 'anti' in Greek can signify two things. It can mean 'against', in which case the word 'antichrist' means an opponent of Christ, or it can mean 'in place of', so that antichrist means a substitute for or a counterfeit of Christ. It is very likely that the ambiguity was intentional, because from its earliest days the Christian church was taught to expect the emergence of a manifestation of evil before Christ's return which would be characterised by both these things. On the one hand, he would be ruthlessly hostile to the Christian faith. On the other hand, he would offer a subtle alternative to it, so that he would be the Antichrist in both senses of the word: a persecutor and a rival.

The precise nature of this mysterious figure is never clearly spelled out. Various phrases are used. Jesus calls him 'the abomination that causes desolation' (Mt 24:15, Mk 13:14), a phrase drawn from the prophecy of Daniel, suggesting some appalling act of sacrilege. Paul in 2 Thessalonians chapter 2 calls him the 'man of lawlessness', depicting a tyrannical individual who commands unconditional obedience from the masses who are deceived by his supernatural charisma. While John in the book of Revelation symbolises him as 'the beast', an incarnation of diabolical power and intelligence, this time in the shape of a political and economic system of oppression.

In these verses, however, the antichrist motif is taken one stage further as it is welded into the theme of last-time apostasy within the church. John is reminding them that they have all heard about the Antichrist that is coming and false prophecy, which is going to be a feature of the last times within the church. He tells them not to think of the two as unconnected because, in reality, they are part of a single demonic stratagem characteristic not just of the days immediately before the end, but of the entire period between Christ's ascension and his return.

So, in 2:18, John writes that antichrist is not just a single individual, because many antichrists have come. Again in 4:3 he emphasises that the coming of the Anti-

christ is not just a particular event: 'This is the spirit of the
Antichrist, which you have heard is coming and even now
is already in the world.'

In other words, antichrist is a principle that manifests
itself in all kinds of ways throughout history. Sometimes it
shows itself as an act of appalling sacrilege that scan-
dalises Christian sensitivity: 'the abomination that causes
desolation'. At other times it appears as a person of terrible anti-Christian influence in the world: 'the man of
lawlessness'. While again, at others, it is seen as an ideo-
logical system dedicated to the extermination of the
church: 'the beast' of Revelation.

Perhaps before the end there will be one great cata-
clysmic antichrist figure who will embody all these things,
but, says John, what we have to realise is that the Antichrist is still at work in the world, even when there are no
gross, obvious, public, personal or political expressions of
his maliciousness. Indeed, the times when the church
appears to be safe and most prosperous are probably the
most dangerous in this regard, because it is then that our
guard slips. The Antichrist moves in to manifest himself
not as an external foe but as an internal one and that,
according to John, is exactly what was happening at the
end of the first century in Asia.

'I am writing these things to you about those who are
trying to lead you astray' (2:26).

He is referring again to the gnostic false teachers and if
up to this point we have felt that John's attitude towards
them has been unnecessarily severe, perhaps we can now
begin to realise why he has been so uncompromising. His
apostolic discernment could detect a deeply sinister
dimension to the activities of these particular heretics.
They were not innocently deluded, the representatives of a
different Christian tradition whose theological insights
can enrich our own. On the contrary, these are agents of
the Antichrist and their emergence is part of a devilish

plot to destroy the church, not by persecution as sometimes happened in the early days, but by sabotage.

The lie

John specifies two things about them that constituted such
a threat: the content of the lie they told and its source.

'Who is the liar? It is the man who denies that Jesus is
the Christ. Such a man is the Antichrist—he denies the
Father and the Son' (2:22).

Previously John has been principally concerned with
the moral consequences of these gnostic ideas, or rather
their lack of them, but, at last, he begins to give us a
clearer picture of the precise nature of their erroneous
teaching. It concerns no less central an issue than the
person of Jesus Christ himself.

Putting the evidence in these passages with what we
know about Gnosticism from extra biblical sources, we
can gain a reasonable idea of what these heretics were in
fact saying. In essence, they were trying to drive a wedge
between Jesus and Christ, saying that Jesus was an ordinary human being and that Christ was a non-material,
divine emanation which temporarily dwelt in him, probably from the time of his baptism in the Jordan until just
before the cross. It is because they refused to accept a total
identification between Jesus and Christ that John says of
them they denied that Jesus was the Christ and because
they refused to accept the unique relationship between
Jesus and God, he adds that they denied the Father and
the Son. Most fundamental of all, they refused to accept
the orthodox doctrine of the Incarnation. That is why
John writes later on: 'Every spirit that acknowledges that
Jesus Christ has come in the flesh is from God' (4:2).

These were the opinions put about by Cerinthus (whom
we have already met), while in the second century there
was even a gnostic sect, the Ophites, who actually

required their disciples to say as part of their creed, 'Jesus is cursed'! It is incredible that a pseudo-Christian group could actually make that their creed, but they did. They were not saying that *Christ* is cursed. They were just cursing the evil bodily encumbrance which Christ had been forced to occupy for a time, named Jesus.

Its source

It may be hard to believe that such a gross distortion of the gospel could ever gain credence in the church, but John tells us the source of their teaching: 'Dear friends, do not believe every spirit, but test the spirits to see whether they are from God, because many false prophets have gone out into the world' (4:1).

These gnostics based their teaching on what they claimed were new revelations from the Spirit of God. It is important to realise that ecstatic utterance, prophecy if you like, is a recurrent feature of many, many world religions. You find it in Hinduism and Islam as well as in Christianity. The Hellenistic world of John was more familiar than most with ecstatic utterance, because many of the mystery religions that were very popular then made it one of their features. We know from the evidence of Corinthians that ecstatic speech was a regular feature of public worship in the early Christian church, whether in an intelligible language, the gift of prophecy as it was called, or in an unintelligible one, the gift of tongues.

The problem is that it is very easy for people to be dazzled by that kind of phenomenon. The fact that pagan religions produce just as much if not more ecstatic experience than Christianity gets forgotten in the intoxicating sense of divine immediacy that the prophet engenders. All discernment collapses and the congregation eagerly swallows everything he says as words unquestionably direct from the mouth of God himself.

It was this appetite for supernatural phenomena such as ecstatic utterance, that the gnostics seemed to be exploiting for their own advantage. If they appealed to the words and the teaching of Jesus and the apostles at all, it was very selectively and with very little regard for their original meaning. Rather, their principal authority lay in the direct experience of the Spirit which they claimed to possess and of which their mystical ecstasies in the congregation provided some plausible evidence, at least to simple-minded Christians in the Hellenistic world who were impressed by such performances.

As we saw earlier, the real problem does not lie in people's scepticism, but in their gullibility. One could wish that people were a lot more sceptical than they are sometimes. 'Do not believe every spirit,' says John. Those who think that Christianity is all about faith, and that believing is always a good thing, irrespective of what one believes in, are sadly mistaken.

These gnostics were completely overturning the major component of orthodox Christian belief—the doctrine of the person of Jesus—by claiming direct vertical access to God through revelatory experience of the Spirit, and far too many of their hearers were accepting what they said without question. That, of course, is a story one could parallel over and over again in the history of the church.

Many of the heretical sects and cults that have sprung up in the last hundred years take issue over the doctrine of the deity of Jesus. Jehovah's Witnesses are an obvious example, but one which is probably more pertinent to these gnostics is Theosophy, or Rosicrucianism as it is sometimes called. This teaches exactly the same separation between Jesus and the Christ that these gnostics did. Theosophy is Gnosticism reborn in the twentieth century. Indeed, you find the same idea in some contemporary Eastern mystical groups.

Back in the 1970s one young guru hit the newspaper headlines by claiming he was Christ. Many people misunderstood him completely, thinking he was purporting to be Jesus returned from the dead, which of course he was not. He was simply claiming to be another reincarnation of the Christ's Spirit, just like Krishna and all the rest of the Hindu pantheon according to him.

At a more academic and sophisticated level, it is possible to identify a very similar attitude towards the person of Christ in the teachings of many modern liberal theologians. They too drive a line of distinction between the Jesus of history and the Christ of faith. They tend to be sceptical of God in the flesh, as is evident, for example, in the book by a group of Anglican scholars, *The Myth of God Incarnate*.[4] The source of these twentieth-century heretical denials of Jesus' deity is in almost every case the same as it was for the gnostics. It is the conviction that the Holy Spirit still has something new to say through a modern prophet, an ecstatic experience or superior theological insight; that the Lord has yet more light and truth to break forth, not from his word, but by special delivery from heaven. 'Be warned,' says John, 'for that is the hallmark of the Antichrist.'

This kind of opposition to the truth is to be expected today because it is a mark of the last times. We must not be surprised by it; still less must we be duped by it. It is part of an unrelenting demonic campaign to destroy the church. If he cannot undermine our life style, he will undermine our doctrine—that is the strategy of the Antichrist. Jesus himself warned us of it and it is the urgent duty of the church in every generation to identify the Antichrist, his lie and his wiles, and to refuse to be seduced by it. Gullibility is something we dare not embrace.

The mark of the true believer: allegiance to the truth

To help us discern an error when it presents itself to us, John gives us three tests by which any Christian can evaluate the truth-claims of would-be teachers in the church and expose the lie for what it is.

Test one: personal experience

'But you have an anointing from the Holy One, and all of you know the truth' (2:20).

Scholars have debated exactly what John means by 'anointing'. Perhaps the most obvious interpretation is that it refers to the gift of the Holy Spirit. That would make sense because in the Gospel of John Jesus does talk about the Holy Spirit 'guiding into all truth' (16:13). But the problem with that interpretation is that it seems to go against the general tenor of what John has been saying. It was the gnostics who relied upon mystical promptings. They were the ones who claimed to have inside knowledge by direct line from the Holy Spirit, and it would seem inconsistent for John to be appealing to this same kind of subjectivism in defence against them. So, many scholars look for other interpretations.

Another possible interpretation is that it signifies baptism. This too is plausible, as we know from early church documents that baptism became associated with a ceremony of anointing in some Christian circles very early on.

Another interpretation refers to the catechism, the elementary Christian teaching which a baptismal candidate received in the early church. The evidence in the text to support that is the correspondence between verses 24 and 27. Verse 24 says, 'See that what you have heard from the beginning remains in you.' And verse 27 says, 'The anointing you received from him remains in you.'

So it is not impossible that 'what you have heard from the beginning' is 'the anointing'. In all likelihood, we do not have to choose among these various understandings of 'the anointing', for the solution probably lies in asking why John uses this extraordinary phrase at all; it is not a common New Testament expression.

Almost certainly, he is echoing the vocabulary of the gnostics. We know from writings of the second century they called the mystical experience which was the kernel of their religion the anointing. So it is likely that what John is doing here is reminding his Christian readers that they too have been anointed. In fact, that is how the New English Bible renders the verse. 'You have had all the spiritual initiation, all the spiritual experience, you need,' John is saying. 'You had it in conversion, in your baptism, in your catechism, in the gift of the Holy Spirit. This was your anointing. You do not need to feel inferior to these spiritual know-it-alls. For you know the truth and in your case the claim is a genuine one. For your anointing is not counterfeit, it is real.'

In other words what John is arguing for here is the competence of every Christian, no matter how humble, to discern the lie by recognising its essential inconsistency with his own conversion experience. He is defending what the Reformers called 'the right of private judgement': 'As for you, the anointing you received from him remains in you, and you do not need anyone to teach you' (2:27).

It is not difficult to see how a verse like that could be abused. History has produced many Christian schismatics who have zealously opposed the infallibility of the Pope, only to install their own personal infallibility in its place by maintaining that they did not need anyone to teach them. John is not saying here that every Christian gets his doctrine by direct hotline from heaven, which is what the gnostics claimed. Indeed, if he had thought that, there would have been no need for him to write this letter. For

that matter, there would have been no need for a New
Testament at all!

Rather, John is appealing here to us as Christians to
live in the light of that initial experience by which we
found God's grace, and not to be seduced by the occult
quest for new experiences. God has nothing more to give
us than Christ, and he gave us him at conversion. All our
spiritual development is a deepening of that relationship
which has been given to us. If we realise that, our Christian intuition will discern the presence of antichrists for,
one way or another, they will subtly be telling us that our
conversion was not enough, that one needs something
extra, something special.

Test two: apostolic doctrine

> This is how you can recognise the Spirit of God: Every
> spirit that acknowledges that Jesus Christ has come in the
> flesh is from God, but every spirit that does not acknow-
> ledge Jesus is not from God. This is the spirit of the
> Antichrist (4:2,3).

These two verses are very significant because in them
John is giving us a primitive creed: 'Jesus Christ has come
in the flesh.' Anyone who claims to have a gift of prophecy
but who cannot assent to that confession of faith, he says,
is not a prophet of God, but of the Antichrist. In other
words, John here is fixing doctrinal criteria by which
Christian orthodoxy can be reliably assessed, even in the
face of those who claim divine authority for their own
teachings.

I want you to notice that he does not outlaw prophetic
utterance from the church. There are some opponents of
the charismatic movement who may wish he had done
that, but it is significant that he does not. For John is no
enemy of charismatic gifts of utterance. It is clear that he

wants to allow for the Holy Spirit's speaking through individuals in the congregation if that is the Spirit's wish.

Nor does he lay down rules about the mode of prophetic delivery, as if the manner of the prophet distinguished falsehood from true. He does not say, for instance, that if the prophet speaks in ecstasy, he is obviously false, but if he speaks in a sober, rational way, then he is true.

Nor is there any form of words that can act as a diagnostic test. He does not say that if the prophet prefixes his prophecy with 'thus saith the Lord', it is accredited and if he does not, it is discredited. For the spirit of the Antichrist can mimic all outward features of prophecy. That is why Jesus called the false prophet the wolf in sheep's clothing. There is no external test by which you can identify him. The test, to John, is doctrinal. The teaching of the true spokesman of God will conform to the apostolic norm.

As far as the gnostic controversy is concerned, the true spokesman of God will acknowledge that Jesus is the Christ come as a true incarnation in the flesh. Notice how the creed there has been formulated by John so as to exclude the gnostics. He has chosen his words specifically with that in mind. In earlier years this would have been a clumsy and an unnecessarily complex creed. 'Jesus is Lord', is all that was needed then, but as the lie becomes increasingly subtle, so the church's confession of faith must become increasingly complex.

This process of defining the church's creed in order specifically to define the heretic is something that continued through the early centuries of the church. It had to. The confessions and creeds grew as the need for orthodoxy to defend itself against the lie grew. It is a necessary evolution of theological definition.

There are churches today that make great play of the fact that they have no confessional statements. Their church members do not have to give assent to any creed, nor do their preachers have to sign any statement of faith.

'We just rely on the Holy Spirit to lead us,' they say. John the apostle would not have approved, for such a policy is an invitation to the Antichrist. It was John and his fellow apostles who gave the impetus to the development of credal statements and without them, humble Christians would find it much harder to distinguish the preacher of truth from the propagator of the lie.

Test three: godly contemporaries

> They are from the world and therefore speak from the viewpoint of the world, and the world listens to them. We are from God, and whoever knows God listens to us; but whoever is not from God does not listen to us. This is how we recognise the Spirit of truth and the spirit of falsehood (4:5,6).

The gnostics were so successful, John explains here, because they were simply an echo of secular attitudes. They are from the world and so they speak from its viewpoint. Take their loose moral attitudes, for instance. The Hellenistic world was renowned for its sexual licence. Prostitution and homosexuality were not even regarded as vices. Gnosticism just reflected the permissive culture of which it was a part.

The same is true of their dualistic attitude that material is essentially evil and the spirit is essentially good. Platonic philosophy had been inculcating precisely that kind of presupposition into the Greek mind for centuries. The gnostics were simply reflecting the opinions of their age.

There is nothing novel, either, about their enthusiasm for mystical experience. The Hellenistic world in the first century was reacting strongly against the intellectualism of Greek rationalism, and enthusiastic mystery cults were springing up all over the place, offering mystical experiences just like those of the gnostics. Everybody was looking for mystical experience in the first century.

At no point did the gnostics require anybody to change. There was no message of repentance in their gospel, and here again they were just exploiting the popular vogue.

Many sociologists argue that that is all religion ever does, that it is the function of religion to endorse the status quo by investing secular values with sacred meaning. If we are honest, we have to acknowledge that a great deal of religion, including much so-called Christianity, has given little evidence to refute that interpretation. But John is convinced that authentic Christianity is different in that it swims against the tide. It is not a rubber stamp on the world's agenda. Nor is it what Francis Schaeffer calls 'an echo of the world'. On the contrary, it witnesses to the unchanging truth of God. This, writes John, is how his readers will be able to tell the Spirit of truth from the spirit of lie.

They need to look at the audience and ask what the people who attend these gnostic meetings are looking for in their religion. Are they embracing this strange teaching because they share in the values, ethics and attitudes of God? Can they see in them a reflection of the qualities of the apostles? Does their life style contradict the world? To put it bluntly, is there something a little odd about them?

John is not encouraging bizarre or eccentric behaviour among Christians, but a community that is really on God's side is always going to appear a little unusual to the man in the street. For, as Jesus said, 'They are not of the world, even as I am not of it' (Jn 17:16). If that trace of oddness, that swimming against the tide is there, one has a strong presupposition that the Spirit of truth is at work there.

'They went out from us, but they did not really belong to us' (2:19).

It seems that at least one gnostic group had voluntarily separated from the main congregation to whom John is writing. Schism in the church is always a sad affair, but sometimes it is inevitable, because the church is the pillar and bulwark of the truth and cannot long harbour ambassadors of the lie. They went out into the world, says John, because that is where they belonged. They are popular because they appeal to popular taste. The church is derided and disdained because it refuses to be borne along on the bandwagon of contemporary culture. It refuses to honour the spirit of the age. It is committed to the Spirit of truth.

There are many things which are conservative and traditionalist about evangelical churches in this country and which irk a modern young person, often rightly so. But if it is a choice between old-fashioned truth and contemporary error, I am happy to be out of date. I do not excuse the church's obstinate traditionalism, but there are things which are more important than being modern. It is the characteristic of heretical groups that they solicit modernity and demonstrate their unwillingness to recognise the truths of that old-time religion, the unchanging values of God.

Chapter 5

Holiness

1 John 2:28–3:10

An out-of-date concept?

For many people today, holiness has definitely negative
connotations. Holiness is that ethereal remoteness that
makes you fidget uncomfortably in a Gothic cathedral. It
is that embarrassed silence that descends on the railway
compartment when a party of nuns enters. Holiness is that
disdainful glare that the zealous church-goer gives you
when he sees you washing your car on Sunday. In short,
for most people holiness is boring. It is killjoy; pompous.
It is certainly not something that the average man or
woman in the street would list among their ten highest
priorities.

You must have some failings to be human. To seek to
live a life of superlative goodness is unnatural, neurotic,
unhealthy, cranky. To quote CD Broad: 'A moderate
appetite for respectability kept within bounds by common
sense and good manners is acceptable. But to hunger and
thirst for righteousness, that is a symptom of diabetes.'

Even among Christians, the same unwillingness to
aspire to holiness percolates through. The saints are
exalted into semi-mythical figures who stare down at us
from stained-glass windows, safely divorced from the daily

routine of living. We do not perhaps despise holiness in quite the way the world generally does—indeed, we may even admire it, from a safe distance—but sheer humility makes it inconceivable that we should ever make it a personal goal. Even for Christians, holiness is widely regarded as an abnormality, an exception to the rule.

If we regard holiness like that as something eccentric and even undesirable, the section of the first letter of John to which we now come has something to teach us because, contrary to our contemporary lack of enthusiasm for it, John tells us here that holiness is in fact absolutely necessary for any who want to call themselves Christian.

As we have seen, John's interest in this question of moral conduct arises from his concern to counter the false teaching of gnostics who had invaded the church. One of the results of their erroneous ideas was an attitude of moral permissiveness. 'Oh!' they said, 'your body is irredeemably evil. The spirit inside it is good. So what you do with your body is a matter of no consequence. The really advanced Christian can sin all he likes and he does not sustain any inward spiritual harm as a result.'

If they had been with us today, their arguments would probably have been slightly different. They would have talked about bodily appetites being 'natural', about chastity breeding Freudian repression, about the Ten Commandments being outmoded by Jesus' ethic of love and so on. Yet, though the arguments have changed over the centuries, the practical consequences are as perennial as couch-grass. It is tough to be holy, so the human race has never been short of plausible excuses for not having to be bothered about it. The gnostics are just one example of the habitual tendency in us as human beings to rationalise moral failure, one way or another.

This will not do, however, for the apostle John. In this passage he is concerned to give us three reasons why every Christian, not just some super-spiritual élite destined for canonisation, must seek to live a life of perfection and to be satisfied with nothing less.

Who we are

'How great is the love that the Father has lavished on us, that we should be called children of God!' (3:1).

A little boy was being teased at school because he was adopted. He suffered the gibes of his class-mates patiently for a while and then he blurted out in fierce self-defence: 'You can say what you like. All I know is that my parents *chose* me. Yours couldn't help having you!' Of course, he was right. Understood that way, an adoption is not a disgrace but a privilege. In a world strewn with unhappy and unwanted children, the adopted child knows that he was no unfortunate intrusion into the life of his mother and father. They had a free choice and they elected to call him their son. If that is true of those adopted by human parents, how much more true is it of Christians, who have been called the children of God!

There is an atmosphere of astonishment and exclama-tion exuding from this opening verse of chapter 3. Liter-ally John says, 'Behold what an extraordinary love!' The word suggests something exotic and mysterious that comes from a distant country. Cinderella had the help of a fairy-godmother to make her beautiful, but our Prince saw us in our rags and still loved us. Do we really appreciate the wonder of that? We sing such hymns as John Newton's 'Amazing Grace', but has it really dawned on us how amazing it is that we should be called the children of God?

What is more, John goes on to explain that this new identity within the family of God is no mere formal title. It is not just a certificate that one pins on the wall. There has been a real change in our practical experience too. We are called the children of God because that is in fact what we are.

Many people are sceptical when we tell them that, as Christians, we enjoy a personal relationship with God. They call us cranks and fanatics. But that, according to John, is what they called Jesus. They did not recognise his divine sonship either, but it was real just as our adoption is real. It is a reality in our hearts now, and one day that reality will become apparent to everybody.

> Dear friends, now we are children of God, and what we will be has not yet been made known. But we know that when he appears, we shall be like him, for we shall see him as he is (3:2).

Mystical experiences

Medieval Catholic mystics spoke often of the so-called 'beatific vision' of God. Teresa of Avila in the sixteenth century, for example, quite explicitly claimed to have direct visual experiences of Christ in the context of her devotional ecstasy. If we are disposed to be sceptical about such claims, it is as well to remember that several biblical writers offer similar testimony. John on the Isle of Patmos, Isaiah in the temple, Ezekiel by the riverside, all speak of visions of God, and there does not seem to be any particular reason to limit the occurrence of such experience to apostles and prophets.

The problem with such experiences is not that they are poorly accredited—and hence of dubious authenticity—but that they are in no way unique to Christianity. Every religion in the world has its mystic visionaries, and the gnostics, whom John is so concerned to combat, are no exception. Indeed, the beatific vision was central to their religious consciousness. In all probability they advertised the particular psychedelic initiation they were peddling at the end of the first century as a way of seeing God, and even of being deified in the process. That being so, it is

important to take note of two things that John has to say
in this context.

'Not yet'

First of all he tells us that there is a 'not yet' about the
Christian vision of God. 'What we will be has not yet been
made known,' he says. The gnostics, on the other hand,
had no interest in waiting for blessings. Theirs was a
religion of immediate gratification. They offered a direct
vertical pipe-line to paradise that could be tapped at once
and as often as desired.

John does not deny the validity of the mind-blowing
mystical experiences they talked about, but implies clearly
here that they are not the Christian norm, as they are not
even the real substance of Christianity. For the fact is that
the Christian's experience in this world is necessarily limited and incomplete because there is a barrier of ignorance
he cannot breach.

As Paul says in his first letter to the Corinthians, 'We
know in part' (13:9). Our perception and experience of
God is at best a poor reflection in an imperfect mirror.
Those who pretend that by some mystical experience they
can disperse the cloud of unknowing and, like Alice, go
through the looking glass into direct, immediate perception of God as he is, are deluding themselves.

Even when mystical experience is a genuine God-given
thing, it can never be anything more than a gracious
accommodation of God to the limitations of our imagina-
tions. We cannot see God as he is—it would be like
looking at the sun with our naked eyes. No man can see
God and live.

Rather, says John, we shall see God, but not as we are
and not in this world. That supreme beatific vision of
unveiled deity is not to be found in private, subjective
ecstasies, but by patiently waiting for the public and
objective return of Christ. When he appears, we shall see

him as he is. And until that climactic event, we must accept a 'not yet' in our experience.

The moral implication

The second thing that John has to say about seeing God is that for the Christian it has moral implications.

'We shall be like him, for we shall see him as he is. Everyone who has this hope in him purifies himself' (3:2,3).

When he says, 'We shall be like him,' John is not of course suggesting that God intends to populate heaven with millions of clones of Jesus Christ. It is one of the most distinctive features of the Christian hope that individual personality is preserved in eternity. We are not going to be dissolved into some impersonal soup of spiritual energy which is what Hindus and Buddhists believe. Nor are we going to be moulded into the stereotyped uniformity of the classless society, as Marx would have it. It is the moral likeness of Christ that John is speaking of here. The diversity of the human race is not in question. We shall share Jesus' sinlessness on that day.

If that seems inconceivable to us because we have difficulty imagining ourselves sinless, why should it? That is what we were made for in the first place. When God created us, he formed us in his own image. Jesus, the righteous one, is the prototype on which our human race was originally modelled. He is *the* normal human being; sociologists and psychologists take note!

This is where those who suggest that one has to be a bit of a sinner to be a truly human person are so wide of the mark. Sin is not human, but subhuman, a tragic falling short of our true dignity. The irony of Adam is that in striving to become like God, he became less than man, and the purpose of the whole plan of salvation is nothing less than the recovery of our true humanity. To be conformed to the image of God's Son is what it is all about and, anybody who has that expectation in front of them lives differently: 'Everyone who has this hope in him purifies himself, just as he is pure' (3:3).

Perfection is your destiny, Christian, and the anticipation of that surely demands that we make progress towards perfection here and now. As John puts it in verses 28 and 29 at the end of chapter 2:

> Continue in him, so that when he appears we may be confident and unashamed before him at his coming. If you know that he is righteous, you know that everyone who does what is right has been born of him.

If we knew that the Queen was coming to our house, we would want to make sure that everywhere was clean and tidy. I remember when President Kenyatta of Kenya was going to visit a town, the inhabitants practically repainted every shop and house along the entire route.

Well, John here is talking about a royal visit to end all royal visits. This is the *parousia*. This is *the* arrival of the King. How we would blush to be found by his Majesty King Jesus with cobwebs all over our life! Surely we want to meet him confident and unembarrassed. 'Everyone who has this hope in him purifies himself.'

'Everyone who sins breaks the law; in fact, sin is lawlessness. But you know that he appeared so that he might take away our sins' (3:4,5).

Many commentators regard the definition of sin that John gives here as rather naïve and superficial because, they suggest, it considers wrong-doing just in terms of breaking rules. Yet I find their comment quite inappropriate. I am sure that John did not think of sin in such a narrow way and I am equally sure that the word 'lawlessness' does not imply that he did. Rather, what John is saying here is that the root of all evil is rebellion against God's authority and God's standards.

'Sin is lawlessness'

Contrary to the humanistic claptrap that has infected so much educational theory and criminology, sin is not the product of our genetic inheritance or of our adolescent hormones. It is not excusable on grounds of a deprived upbringing or cultural conditioning. It is not a relic of our evolutionary origins or the artefact of our social development. Sin is fundamentally an attitude of moral anarchy. 'Why should I?' is the question everybody asks. The sulky child weeps it when he is told to put his toys away. The petulant teenager demands it when he is told to do his homework. The irate employee mutters it when he is told to be more punctual. Adam said it when he was told to leave the tree of knowledge alone, and every sinner has said it since then. Sin is the refusal to accept the authority of God over our lives. It is the failure to conform to God's norms for our lives. John rightly terms it lawlessness, because there is no better word to describe it. He then proceeds to describe the origins of this defiant moral autonomy which has its roots deep in our whole personality.

'He who does what is sinful is of the Devil, because the Devil has been sinning from the beginning' (3:8).

We persuade ourselves that our sin frees us from the cramping and inhibiting conventions of bourgeois morality. We live as we please. We do as we like. We are liberated and enlightened members of the permissive society.

John would have us know that we are not free. We are pawns of demonic spiritual forces of which we know nothing. Of course, the Devil is not stupid enough to reveal himself. Unlike God, he does not need us to believe in him before he can work in us. The Devil is no gentleman. He is a spiritual rapist. He awaits an opportunity not an invitation. So long as we mock him as that ridiculous figure with horns and red tights, his control over our behaviour is rendered all the more secure for our being totally unconscious of it. But he is there all right and we will discover the bondage in which he has secretly enthralled us the moment we try to live a holy life. It is true that sin is our choice, but we delude ourselves if we think it is a free choice. No, sin is our habit, our nature, our slavery.

The whole universe is in a state of cosmic civil war. It has been ever since the emergence on this planet of the human race, possibly even longer. John tells us that the Devil has been sinning since the beginning, and our personalities are now enemy occupied territory. That is our problem and that is why Jesus came. If we had been capable of perfection through our own efforts, there would have been no need for such an extraordinary stratagem on God's part. He could have managed without Jesus; we would have no need of a Saviour. But the fact is as things stand, we have no hope without one!

Like a computer in a science-fiction thriller, the universe is in the perverted grip of an evil hacker, and it needs somebody to come in from outside to emancipate us from that program loop of wickedness in which we are so helplessly confined. This, John writes, is why Jesus appeared, in order to take away sin. 'The reason the Son of God appeared was to destroy [or a better translation, 'to loose from bondage'] the Devil's work' (3:8).

It is very important that we understand this. Jesus did not come primarily as a teacher to improve our moral education, but as a sacrifice to make atonement for our lawlessness. Jesus did not come primarily as an example to demonstrate the way of love, but as a warrior to win a victory over spiritual hosts of wickedness and to liberate us from their power. The entire purpose of Jesus was to overcome the power of sin in our lives. That being so, John asks how we can possibly continue to surrender to it:

'No one who lives in him keeps on sinning. No one who continues to sin has either seen him or known him' (3:6).

As the Puritan divine John Owen puts it, 'Did Christ die and shall sin live?' Every sin a Christian commits he knows adds directly to the burden Christ bore on the cross. Every failure to conform to God's standards denies the spiritual victory Jesus won there and grants the Devil grounds for hope. Nobody who understands why Christ came can possibly live in anything but a state of unceasing war against sin. Our holiness is the whole object of the Incarnation.

What God has done

'No one who is born of God will continue to sin, because God's seed remains in him; he cannot go on sinning, because he has been born of God' (3:9).

Scholars are divided about what precisely John means by that word 'seed'. Some argue that it is just a Jewish idiom for 'family', and so we should translate the verse 'as God's family remains in him', that is, 'in God'. This interpretation makes sense, but is a rather unnatural rendering of the passage.

Others argue that 'seed' stands for the gospel, because in the parable of the sower, for instance, the seed is the word. Once again, that makes sense, but there is no real clear evidence that that is John's meaning, any more than there is for the third and most popular explanation that the 'seed' is a symbol for the indwelling of the Holy Spirit in the Christian.

All these interpretations have their merits but, as was the case with that other rather cryptic phrase, 'the anointing', that we encountered in chapter 2, the clue to understanding John's meaning is to recognise that here John is probably using the vocabulary of the false teachers and trying to steal their thunder. There is good evidence that the gnostics taught that by means of a mystical vision of God, a human being could actually become divine. They called this process 'being fertilised by the divine seed'!

In that case, what John is demonstrating here is that there is an element of truth in what the gnostics were saying. There is always an element of truth in every powerful lie; there has to be or nobody would ever give it credence. As Christians, we do become partakers of God's nature. Our experience of God is not just a contractual arrangement, it is also a spiritual transformation. He does not merely shake our hands; he regenerates our hearts inwardly. His seed is in us and in a sense that is what makes the analogy of adoption an inadequate one, because in human terms when parents adopt a child, though they may give their child the legal status of being a son or daughter, they cannot actually work the miracle of making that child biologically their own. But God can. When God adopts us into his family, he shares his genes with us. His seed abides in us.

We are given not just a new relationship but a new nature, God's own nature. We are the children of God and, like true children, we grow up to bear the family likeness. This, says John, constitutes the third and perhaps the most powerful reason why Christians must be holy: because sin is fundamentally inconsistent with our new birth: 'No one who is born of God will continue to sin, because God's seed remains in him; he cannot go on sinning, because he has been born of God' (3:9).

Great care needs to be exercised at this point, as there have been some who have interpreted John as teaching here the possibility of attaining sinless perfection in this life. John Wesley, for instance, argued this, although most scholars agree that his thinking is extremely complex, not to say confused, on the subject. Others in the Methodist holiness tradition that Wesley started, such as Charles

Finney, for instance, have been more outspoken. He actually argued that it must be possible for a Christian to be sinless, since it was inconceivable that God would command what men were incapable of performing: 'If Jesus says "be perfect", then surely we must be able to be perfect,' he said.

I have to say that, along with the vast majority of evangelical commentators on this passage, I do not believe that that is what John intended to teach at all!

To deal first with Finney's argument, it is not true that a divine command implies a human ability. That is the Pelagian heresy which the church contested in the Middle Ages. A bankrupt man may owe a million pounds and be incapable of paying a penny. In just the same way, a morally bankrupt human race can be responsible to obey God's whole law and be congenitally incapable of keeping one commandment.

B B Warfield says, 'If we are only to be judged by the subjective standard of our own ability, then it is a case of "where ignorance is bliss, it is folly to be wise."'

The more morally incompetent we are, the better. 'I couldn't help it, Lord, I can resist anything but temptation,' and our defence would be impregnable.

Moreover, if John is intending here to argue for sinless perfection, then verse 9 proves far too much, for it implies not just that *some* Christians may succeed in overcoming sin completely, but that sin is an impossibility for *every* Christian. 'No one who is born of God will continue to sin,' he says. So, if he is trying to teach sinless perfection, he teaches it for everybody from the beginning, and I do not think any perfectionist has wanted to argue that. In any case, sinless perfection is inconsistent with the rest of this letter. As we noted when we were considering chapter 1: 'If we claim to be without sin, we deceive ourselves…. If we claim we have not sinned, we make him out to be a liar and his word has no place in our lives' (1:8,10).

John even goes out of his way to make plain to Christians the ongoing cleansing from sin which God has provided for us as the way of escape when we sin: 'But if anybody does sin, we have one who speaks to the Father in our defence—Jesus Christ, the Righteous One. He is the atoning sacrifice for our sins' (2:1,2). Are we to believe that John implies that we will get to the point where we no longer need the intercession of Jesus or the blood of Jesus?

More than that, sinless perfection is inconsistent with the rest of the Bible. In the Lord's Prayer, for example, we are instructed to pray: 'Forgive us our sins' (Lk 11:4). It is inconceivable that Jesus would have taught his disciples to make such a clause a regular part of their devotional life if he intended that confession of sin should become a redundant exercise.

Most significant of all, sinless perfection is totally inconsistent with Christian experience, for the greatest saints have never claimed sinlessness. As the hymn says,

> And they who fain would serve thee best
> Are conscious most of wrong within.[5]

You have only to read the penitential psalms of David to realise that.

While a perfectionist interpretation of verse 9 raises insurmountable objections, the problem of establishing what John does mean by this very strong statement remains.

Some have argued that by 'sinning' here John is just meaning deliberate, gross sin. These are the commentators who suggest that 'lawlessness' in verse 4 just means breaking rules consciously and nothing more. Even if they were right in their evaluation of John's understanding of the word 'sin' there, there would still be problems because verse 9 suggests if that is so, then Christians never sin deliberately. Is that true? Surely, David's adultery and Peter's denial of Christ point to the contrary.

Others maintain that John is only arguing for the sinlessness of our renewed nature, saying that it is the divine seed in us that cannot sin, while our old natures continue to be victims to moral failure. Yet that schizophrenic model of the Christian life is precisely the same dualistic sophistry the gnostics employed when they maintained that the body is sinful and the spirit is righteous. It is inconceivable that John would be answering their challenge by defending that kind of theology of permissiveness. Of course, the flesh and the spirit struggle within a Christian, but not in such a way as to absolve us from blame when the flesh wins out.

Still others have argued that John here is making an idealistic, generalised statement. But I find that unsatisfactory, because it amounts to relegating an infallible statement of Scripture to the realm of vague generalisation and wild exaggeration.

By far the most convincing interpretation of verse 9 is that which takes careful note of the Greek tenses that are involved. All the verbs in verse 9 are in the present tense and in Greek this implies continuity of action. The NIV translation has very properly tried to express that by interpreting it as: 'No one who is born of God will *continue* to sin…he cannot *go on* sinning,' and that contrasts very markedly with chapter 2, verse 1, where John writes: 'I write this to you so that you will not sin. But if anybody does sin, we have one who speaks to the Father in our defence,' because the verbs there are in another tense, which expresses the idea of a single, isolated act.

John's view is that what the seed of God does in the experience of the Christian is to break the habit of sin. It changes the general tenor of our lives from being towards sin to being towards righteousness, with the result that the Christian does not go on sinning as he used to do. He may commit isolated acts of sin, indeed it is inevitable that he

will do so. Sometimes he may so backslide as to do this
quite deliberately as did David. But his renewed conscience will give him no rest in that state of sin, because
the divine nature within him will draw him to repentance,
even though the inner struggle may be immensely painful.
To use a phrase John Stott employs in his commentary, it
is not the impossibility of sin that John is arguing for, but
the incongruity of it.[6]

In the first place it is incongruous because we are the
adopted children of God, destined for glory. The second
reason is that Christ came to redeem us, not just from the
penalty of sin but from its power also. Most of all it is
incongruous because of the regeneration that God has
worked in our hearts, implanting his own divine nature
within our souls. Holiness is not an optional extra, but the
Christian norm.

A vital lesson

It is vital that we grasp the importance of holiness, for
John tells us here that our assurance of salvation depends
upon it:

> This is how we know who the children of God are and who
> the children of the Devil are: Anyone who does not do
> what is right is not a child of God; nor is anyone who does
> not love his brother (3:10).

It was the great Augustine who said in his *Confessions*,
'Give me chastity and self-restraint, but do not give it yet.'
Shortly, he would be holy, he said, but his shortly grew
into a greatly and his little while lengthened into a long
while for, he added, 'I did not want my lust quenched but
rather glutted.'[7]

We can all be guilty of putting off our sanctification, or
delaying the pursuit of holiness. Having accepted the
salvation Jesus offers, having called ourselves Christians

and entered his church, we can still question whether holiness is really necessary for the Christian, telling ourselves that after all the Bible makes it very clear that one cannot be saved by good works, that it is all dependent on God's free mercy: 'By grace you have been saved...not by works' (Eph 2:8,9).

John's reply to such questions is short and uncompromising: 'No one who is born of God will continue to sin' (3:9). The index of our present spiritual state, whether it is heaven-bound or hell-bound, is our attitude to sin. If we are living immorally today and intend to go on doing so tomorrow, it is no good complaining that we doubt our salvation, that we are feeling spiritually depressed or that the Holy Spirit's witness has fled our heart. We have no right to assurance in such a state.

Indeed, John warns us that our soul is in danger. Regardless of how many decisions we have made, how many testimonies we have given, or how many times we have been to church, if our lives declare that we are under God's wrath, that is the only place we can assume ourselves to be. Mercy is reserved for those who sincerely seek to give up their sins and live for God. To his credit, Augustine knew that so long as he was crying, 'Give me chastity and self-restraint, but...not...yet,' he was unsaved. He knew he could not become a Christian until he could say from his heart, 'Give me chastity and self-restraint, Lord, and give it now,' because Augustine knew that there was no justification from past sins without holiness for present life. He knew he could not boast of Christ's work for him until he could demonstrate Christ's work in him.

It is to our shame that many Christians today, with all our decision cards and our appeals in evangelistic booklets, are sometimes guilty of postponing teaching about the need for holiness until after we have extracted a confession of Christ. Then, as we see sin continuing in someone's life, we call them backsliders and carnal Christians, when the truth is that, until the moral character of God is evident in their lives, there is no ground to call them Christians at all.

The Bible never counsels habitual sinners as Christians, it warns them as reprobates. As William Gurnall, the Puritan preacher, writes, 'Say not thou art born of God and hast the royal blood in thy veins, except thou canst prove thy pedigree by daring to be holy.' Notice what John says about this in verse 7, 'Do not let anyone lead you astray'. There will be clever men who will persuade us we can be Christians and keep our sins, but they are wrong. Holiness is an urgent necessity. We ignore its pursuit at our spiritual peril. That is how serious, how important it is. It is priority number one.

Chapter 6

Love

1 John 3:11–24; 4:7–21

Love is...

I strongly suspect that if you were to conduct a word association test with a random sample of modern men and women, you would find that the first idea that springs into most people's minds at the mention of the word love is sex or something related to it.

This might not be particularly serious if it were simply a development in English usage. After all, words are changing their meaning all the time; but, at the risk of being labelled puritanical, I have to say I think there is more to it than that. There seem to me to be clear signs that Western society generally is becoming little short of obsessed with the sexual dimension of love and that this is blurring our idea about love altogether.

In his book 'The Making of the Modern Family' (Collins, 1976) the sociologist, Edward Shorter, actually cites evidence for this. He compares the famous Kinsey report on sexual behaviour that came out in the 1940s with a much more recent survey conducted in the 1970s by Morton Hunt. He draws the conclusion that there has been an 'eroticisation' of Western society in the last thirty years. Shorter points out that sexual expectations have risen enormously. As a result, the importance that people attribute to sexual fulfilment is at an unprecedented level, and he reckons that this is one contributory factor in the increased incidence of marital breakdown.

Blame it on Freud, Hollywood, or whoever you like, it is clear to any observer that everything in our culture today, from pop music to chocolate advertisements, is charged with eroticism. The narrowing of our definition of love is simply one more indication of that trend.

The romanticism of the early twentieth century used to talk about falling in love. Now the sensualism of the late twentieth century talks about making love. It is a regrettable trend, because it means that many subtle and noble aspects of human experience are becoming obscured or even rendered inexpressible. Aldous Huxley anticipated this when in *Brave New World* he depicted the artistic and literary impoverishment that accompanies a culture where love and sex become synonymous.

More immediately, it raises a problem for us in our understanding of 1 John, because there is no theme more central to the apostle's interest than that of love. The noun and the verb together are used nearly fifty times in these five brief chapters. Some of John's statements about love are among the most memorable and moving in the entire Bible. Yet, powerful and appealing as the thoughts of John on this subject of love are, I believe that there is a serious danger that we shall completely misunderstand what he means, because we read his words through the filter of our contemporary eroticised culture.

Let me give you an example of what I mean. Some years ago I was in a Bible study with a group of mainly young people and we were looking at this very passage that we now come to consider. We reached verse 16: 'God is love. Whoever lives in love lives in God, and God in him' (4:16).

'Can anybody tell us what that means?' the leader of the Bible study asked. Whereupon one rather intense young lady, sitting opposite me, burst out, 'Oh yes, I think I have experienced it. Sometimes in my quiet time I'm just bowled over by Jesus's love. It reduces me to tears. Jesus is so wonderful, I feel as if the whole room is bathed in love.'

I can't remember her precise words but it was something like that and her startling testimony stupified the rest of the Bible study group for a good thirty seconds. What occupied my thoughts during that stunned silence was how similar her description of her experience of God's love was to that which you might expect from some romantic love song about a girl who is 'in heaven' having just fallen madly for some young man.

What had happened was that she had seen the word 'love' in 1 John 4, had read into it all the romantic overtones which that word conjures up in a twentieth century mind, and had then identified it with a particularly rapturous experience of God she had enjoyed in her private devotions.

While I am sure that that experience of Christ she spoke about was genuine, I am equally sure that her interpretation of 1 John 4:16 was completely false. The first thing we must do if we are to grasp what John wants to teach us about love is to get a clear and accurate idea of what he means by the word. We need a definition of love that will deliver us from the bias towards love between the sexes which all our contemporary definitions of love tend to encourage.

The word John uses

It must be regarded as one of the minor providences of the Bible that the Greek language has no less than four distinct words covering the range of meaning which in

English is embraced by the single word 'love'. This means that Greek statements about love are nowhere near as imprecise or open to misunderstanding as their corresponding English translations. One of those four words means sexual love. Predictably, in our twentieth century, it is one of the few Greek words most of us know: *eros*.

Eros

It is important to realise that it is perfectly imaginable that *eros* could have been the word John chose to use here in 1 John 4, because it had a religious significance. It was in fact part of the vocabulary of mystical experience.

Plato, the philosopher, had probably been the catalyst for this sense of the word when, some four hundred years before Jesus, he used the word *eros* in his 'Symposium' to describe the compelling and irresistible attraction of divine things. Later, in the mystery religions which became popular in Greece, the same word was used to describe the emotional release which mystic initiates enjoyed in the state of religious ecstasy. Indeed, that mystical strand of religious interest in *eros* is identifiable right through history and across cultures. A classic pagan example of it is the tantric yoga of Hinduism in which sexual intercourse is actually exploited by Eastern gurus as a technique for achieving spiritual enlightenment.

Christianity has never gone that far, because of its strong ethical constraints on sexual behaviour, but it still uses the language of *eros*. Catholic mediaeval mystics often described their experience of mystical union with God in unmistakably erotic language. Any who are familiar with Puritan commentaries on the Song of Solomon will be well aware how often that poetic celebration of God's gift of sexual love has been spiritualised so that it becomes a vehicle for the expression of religious rather than marital devotion. In fact this influence of *eros* language on

protestant piety is detectable in our hymn books. Take, for
example:

> I lift my heart to Thee,
> Saviour divine;
> For Thou art all to me
> And I am Thine.
> Is there on earth a closer bond than this;
> That my Beloved's mine and I am His?

The last line is a direct quotation from the Song of Solomon and originally is the word of a very erotic lover to
his very erotic bride.

This is seen again in the verse of a hymn by George
Robinson:

> Things that once were wild alarms
> Cannot now disturb my rest;
> Closed in everlasting arms,
> Pillowed on the loving breast.
> O to lie for ever here,
> Doubt and care and self resign,
> While He whispers in my ear—
> I am His and He is mine.

But the classic example is Wesley's:

> O love divine how sweet thou art!
> When shall I find my willing heart
> All taken up by thee?
> I thirst, I faint, I die to prove
> The greatness of redeeming love,
> The love of Christ to me.
>
> For love I sigh, for love I pine;
> This only portion, Lord, be mine,
> Be mine this better part!
>
> Oh that I could for ever sit
> With Mary at the Master's feet!

Be this my happy choice;
My only care, delight and bliss,
My joy, my heaven on earth, be this,
To hear the Bridegroom's voice.

Of course, all this is well attested and perfectly valid Christian testimony in verse. Perhaps that girl in my Bible study group had discovered the same thing. There is quite definitely an experience of mystical communion with Christ which is so passionate, so all-consuming, so ecstatic, so climactic, that there is little else one can call it except a spiritual orgasm.

It is small wonder that those who have enjoyed such intensity of emotional involvement with God in their devotional lives have felt drawn to use the language of *eros* to describe it. So if John had chosen to use *eros* to describe the love which characterises God, it would not have surprised or seemed ridiculous either to his own original hearers or to many Christians since. Indeed, it is far from unlikely that the gnostic false teachers who were infiltrating the church in John's day did use such language to describe their spiritual ecstasies, in common with both pagan and Christian mystics down through the ages.

Yet it is important to note that although John seems to have been willing to use elements of mystical terminology and vocabulary in this letter—talking about 'the divine knowledge', 'the divine anointing', 'the divine seed', all probably words that were in the mouths of those gnostic mystics—when it comes to the subject of the divine love, he stops short. Instead of the mystical word *eros*, he chooses a quite different word. A word which, because of its complete absence of sensual overtones, has no clear equivalent in contemporary English at all. The Authorised Version renders it 'charity'. Modern translations, for want of a better word, call it 'love' at the risk of the inevitable misunderstanding that accompanies that word.

Agape

Perhaps the safest thing is to anglicise the original Greek—'God is *agape*'. *Agape* is a practical and unemotional love. There are no rapturous, mystical experiences associated with it. In classical Greek it was a rather vague and colourless word which may have been the reason why John and the other New Testament writers chose it as the Christian word for love. As Oliver Wendell Holmes once said 'love is sparingly soluble in words'. It is an abstract noun and, like all such, gains its meaning from association with the mental images that it sparks off in our minds.

The mental images sparked off by *eros*, even in its religious usage, were nothing like what John meant by love. *Agape*, on the other hand, was sufficiently broad and unspecific for John and the other apostles to invest it with the distinctive Christian meaning that they wanted. We see this happening in the New Testament generally and very specifically in 1 John 3 and 4, where John takes the word for love which was relatively cold and colourless in the mind of his Greek speaking audience and paints a picture beside it which would forever define *agape* in the Christian vocabulary. In so doing he distinguishes it from all other worldly loves and particularly from *eros*.

The example John cites

'This is how we know what love is: Jesus Christ laid down his life for us' (3:16).

Or again: 'This is love (*agape*): not that we loved God, but that he loved us and sent his Son as an atoning sacrifice for our sins' (4:10).

When John says 'God is love', he is not referring to some quasi erotic ecstasy, but to Jesus on the Cross. The image sparked off in his mind by the word *agape* is of a love that makes sacrifices for others: Jesus Christ laid down his life for us.

Eros, whatever virtues it may have, is a word of self-gratification. It is a demanding, craving, hungry love; a love born out of the need of the lover. But *agape* is a word of self-forgetfulness. It is a generous, altruistic, sacrificial love born out of the need of the loved one. In short, *eros* is a love that wants to take and *agape* is one that wants to give. 'This is how we know what agape is: Jesus Christ laid down his life for us...'

'...and we ought to lay down our lives for our brothers.' It is all very well to sing pious hymns about love divine all loves excelling, fixing in us his humble dwelling, but if we think of the love of God merely as ardent feelings of religious sentiment in our quiet times, it may well be that that love has no practical consequences at all in our relationships with people.

In fact, *eros* type experiences of God can actually foster a kind of spiritual introversion, because *eros* is a jealous, possessive love. To use a phrase of Antoine De Sale, 'l'amour est un egoisme a deux'—an egoism of two. The kind of unsociable engrossment in one another which couples sometimes display when they are in love, has a spiritual counterpart. Sometimes those who enjoy enormous emotional involvement in their devotional lives, can be incredibly selfish people. You only have to ask their husbands and wives to find that out. But that is not *agape* love. Jesus is a model for us of one who is willing to give anything and everything for the welfare of others, even life itself.

By its very definition, says John, *agape* makes sacrifices for people, and, more than that, bears the pain of the sin of others. 'This is love: not that we loved God, but that he loved us and sent his Son as an atoning sacrifice for our sins' (4:10).

It often escapes people's attention that the only possible way in which dying can demonstrate love is if that death benefits the loved one in some direct way. I can hardly imagine a man saying to his wife one evening, 'Darling, I love you so much I'm going to prove it by putting a bullet through my brain!' In the same way, it is hard to see any love in the death of Jesus if it is no more than a dramatic gesture. John is telling us that something was achieved by Jesus death: 'he sent his Son as an atoning sacrifice for our sins'.

This is the heart of the gospel. God could not in justice overlook our sins, so he sent Jesus to pay the death penalty to satisfy that justice on our behalf. Why? Because he loved us.

Eros love would not do that, at least not very reliably, because *eros* is an uncontrollable and unpredictable passion, as fickle as Cupid's bow. *Eros* is capable of occasional acts of recklessness, but rarely of sustained courage.

Agape, on the other hand, is a word of duty. It is a responsible, determined love, as constant as the decision of the one who promises it. Jesus is a model for us of one who planned, undertook and executed with unwavering commitment a mission of unimaginable agony for himself in order that we might be forgiven. This, says John, is *agape* love which bears the pain of the sin of others in that way.

Further, John tells us, *agape* is a love that takes the initiative towards others.

'This is love: not that we loved God, but that he loved us' (4:10).

And, again: 'We love because he first loved us' (4:19).

Among all the reasons why the language of *eros* was not adaptable to John's meaning of love, this is the one which is probably decisive. *Eros* spoke of men reaching up to God. That is how Plato and the mystery religions used the word. God is infinitely beautiful, infinitely desirable and *eros* is that human passion that motivates us to transcend the confines of this material world in search of an experience of mystical union with the divine. But that is not what the Cross is all about.

The direction is all wrong. Calvary is about a God who reaches down from heaven to us—not because he saw anything attractive or desirable in us, as *eros* would require. On the contrary, we were by nature his enemies. We were guilty sinners, repulsive to his holiness and deserving only his judgement. Yet this God, of his own free will, unprovoked by any external stimulus or attractiveness, so loved the world that he gave his Son.

That is *agape* love. It needs no aphrodisiac to turn it on. It is a love born out of a heart whose nature and purpose is love; one which, even when it is repudiated and nailed to a cross, says, 'Father, forgive them, for they do not know what they are doing.' It is a love which takes the initiative, and that not in self-seeking passion but in self-denying grace. 'We love because he first loved us.'

I am certainly not suggesting that profoundly emotional experiences of God are illusory. There are plenty of Christians who have testified to such, and each of us in our own way probably, to a greater or lesser extent, has known times of such emotional elevation in our devotional lives. But the vital point to grasp is that John is not talking about that kind of thing here. The gnostics may have been, but not the apostle. When he talks about love he is not talking about *eros* but *agape*, a love born not of the emotions, but of the will; one which is not the product of a super-charged libido, but of a moral decision. This is the love God has shown to us in Jesus, and wants from us as the response of grateful hearts.

The search for experiences

We need to take careful note of what John is saying here because there are many people these days who explore

Christianity in the search for experiences that will turn
them on one way or another. To use a word of John
Donne, they want God to 'ravish' them, to strip them of
their inhibitions, to blow their minds, to flood their senses
with ecstasy, to intoxicate them with joy. They want
Christianity more or less as the LSD freak wants drugs, or
the hippies used to want their gurus—as a method of
expanding their consciousness, to gain a psychedelic high.

Rollo May, the well-known American psychiatrist, has
analysed the popularity of the quest for mystical experience today and concludes it all derives from the fact that
we live in an *eros* orientated society. People are consciously
or unconsciously looking for an *eros* experience of God.
Maybe they will find it. But it is vital we understand that
that kind of mystical experience of God is not normative
for the Christian. Some Christians may have such experiences: others certainly will not; and whether we have them
or not, is nothing to do with the genuineness or otherwise
of our Christianity.

Several factors are involved in whether or not people
have such experiences of God, and if you read the literature of mysticism you quickly identify what they are.
Temperament is one: some people are more psychologically inclined to ecstatic experience than others. Quite a
few students of mystical experience have pointed out that
there is a similarity between that and certain kinds of
profound mental disturbance. Some sceptics of course
would say that all mystical experience is psychotic. While
I do not think we need to agree, it could well be that a
predisposition towards emotional disturbance generally
also predisposes towards emotional experiences of God.

Another factor which is often relevant is personal circumstances. A number of writers about mystical experience suggest that a measure of sexual frustration may be
important. It is certainly true that many of the great

mystics of the church have been those who, either voluntarily or by pressure of circumstances, have embraced a
celibate life-style.

No disparagement is implied in either of these comments. If you had taken Ezekiel, the prophet, to a psychi-
atric hospital he would probably have been diagnosed as
schizoid!

The vital thing to realise is that the kind of overwhelm-
ing experience of God's love which that girl in the Bible
study spoke about, may be very precious to the people
who experience it, but it is not universal. It is not what the
Bible means when it says we must seek to live in love and
in God.

W H Auden, in a fascinating essay on *eros* and mysticism, makes the point that this attempt to universalise
mystical experience and make it into a Christian norm
closely parallels the twentieth century attitude to erotic
experience in marriage. Half the literature, high-brow and
popular, produced in the West during the past four hundred years, has been based on the false assumption that
what is an exceptional experience is, and ought to be, a
universal one. Under its influence many millions of people
have persuaded themselves that they were 'in love', when
really they were nothing of the kind.

I suspect that he is quite right. The kind of wild aban-
donment that is portrayed in love songs and in films is not
what normal marriage is like and there is no quicker way
to the divorce court than to think that it is. Romeo and
Juliet are a rare couple and Shakespeare was right when
he portrayed them as tragic. For that is often what *eros* is.
Marriages based on *eros* and nothing else are precariously
unstable because *eros* is such a fickle passion.

In the same way, those who look for ecstatic experiences with God are on precarious ground. In nine cases
out of ten they are going to be disillusioned, because that
kind of thing is simply not for them. Why should it be?

When the Bible talks about love for God, it is not talking about an *eros* experience, but an *agape* one.

Caring, practical love

I think St John of the Cross must be regarded as the most sensible Christian mystic of all history. This is what he writes:

> All visions, revelations, heavenly feelings and whatever experiences are greater than these, are not worth the least act of humility. For acts of humility are the fruit of that *agape* love which neither values nor seeks itself, which thinks well, not of self, but of others. And for this reason, many souls to whom mystical visions have never come, are incomparably more advanced in the way of perfection than others to whom many such experiences have been given.

It is very important for us to understand that in our twentieth century environment. What are we looking for in our Christian life? Are we going around discontented and frustrated because others seem to have a more emotionally charged relationship with God than we have so far experienced? We should not be so childish. Our spirituality is not determined by the level of adrenalin in our bloodstream when we pray. We should not waste our time fretting after *eros* experiences of God. John tells us the kind of love he wants of us both negatively and positively. In both cases the emphasis is on practical, caring, generous relationships with other people.

What hate does

'This is the message you heard from the beginning: We should love one another. Do not be like Cain, who belonged to the evil one and murdered his brother'

(3:11,12). It is a remarkable observation, you know, that the Bible says that the first baby ever born turned out to be a murderer, with the second one as his victim. According to John, this fundamental polarisation has continued to be characteristic of the human race ever since. There are only two sorts of men, he says: those like Cain and those like Abel; the haters and the lovers. What does hate do?

Hate envies

'Why did he murder him? Because his own actions were evil and his brother's were righteous' (3:12). The early chapters of Genesis that John is referring to here tell us that Cain and Abel both brought an offering to God, but while Abel's was accepted, Cain's was not. We are not given the reason for this divine discrimination, if indeed there is a one beyond the sovereign choice of a God who is not obliged to accept anything from a human hand. Abel was, as we would perhaps want to say, the lucky one.

But according to John, there was a test of moral calibre implicit in the situation. We are told that Cain was 'very angry' when God refused his sacrifice and 'his face was downcast'.

What attitude do we take up when we are confronted by good fortune in other people? How do we feel when we meet the person who is the great business success we always wanted to be, but never were? How do we feel when we meet the fellow who got to university when we failed 'O' levels? How does the single girl feel when she hears that her best friend has just got engaged to a good-looking millionaire? How does the barren woman feel when she hears that her neighbour is going to have a baby?

So often our reaction in these and similar circumstances is simply jealousy—green-eyed envy. But love has another way to deal with the good fortune of others. Love has no pride to be wounded, no ego to be threatened, so it can rejoice in the superiority of others, admiring without resentment, praising without cynicism. 'Love does not envy', but hate does: indeed it does worse.

'Anyone who hates his brother is a murderer' (3:15). Here John implies a moral identification between hate and homicide that you may consider rather far-fetched. While we sometimes say, 'If looks could kill,' mercifully they cannot, or there would be a lot of dead people around. There is a difference between throwing daggers at your neighbour with your eyes, and throwing them literally with your hands. So is it not unreasonable for the Bible to maintain this moral equation that anybody who hates is a killer? Surely losing my temper with somebody does not put me in the dock on a charge of murder. John is saying that, in a very real sense, it does; and it is important that we realise that that thought did not originate with him. Almost certainly, this is a reference to the words of Jesus himself:

> You have heard that it was said to the people long ago, "Do not murder and anyone who murders will be subject to judgment." But I tell that anyone who is angry with his brother will be subject to judgment (Mt 5:21,22).

Murder is the action of a man who sees no value in another human being. As far as he is concerned, the other's existence is so trivial, so unimportant, so worthless that it is dispensable. Murder is an act of contempt, and what Jesus and John are saying is that we demonstrate precisely the same contemptuous disregard for the worth of other human beings when we despise them. As far as God is concerned, hatred and homicide are equally heinous. In heart both bid their neighbour good riddance.

Hate demonises

'Do not be like Cain, who belonged to the evil one' (3:11). Dostoyevsky says, 'Hell is the suffering of being unable to love.' He's right. Hell is ultimate egotism, the antithesis of community.

Hell is a place where men have wrapped themselves up so totally in themselves that their souls have become impenetrable cysts cut off from all external light and love and life by the ceaselessness of their self absorption. Hell is a black hole in the spiritual universe: it can absorb, but can never radiate. For hate can only take, it can never give. Without any shadow of doubt, if we are on Cain's side—the side of envy, murder and hate—then we are also on the side of hell. Hate is what demonises our society.

What love does

Thank God, there is an alternative. 'This is the message you heard from the beginning, we should love one another…This is how we know what love is: Jesus Christ laid down his life for us. And we ought to lay down our lives for our brothers' (3:11,16).

There is a contrast here. Whereas it is the nature of hate to take life, says John, it is the nature of love to surrender life. The Marxist revolution will never create a loving society because its commitment to violence puts it on the side of Cain not of Abel. Jesus demonstrated that the only way to build a community where *agape* prevails was not by wielding a machine gun, but by carrying a cross: not by taking people's lives, but by giving your own. In contrast to envious and murderous hate, love suffers.

Love suffers

'Do not be surprised, my brothers, if the world hates you' (3:13). Occasionally I meet people who are full of resent-

ment and bitterness because Christianity has brought
them nothing but trouble. 'Ever since I became a Christian things have gone worse, not better,' they say. 'It is not
fair. I thought God would solve all my problems. All he
has done is add to them.' But why should we feel cheated
if that is our experience? Jesus did not promise a bed of
roses. He said, 'If the world hates you, keep in mind that it
hated me first' (Jn 17:18).

The world did not treat Jesus well and he was a better
Christian than any of us. It should be no surprise to us if
the way of love is a painful road; it was, too, for the
Master. That is what makes Christian suffering so precious for, when a Christian suffers, God is taking us up
into his own experience. If we feel rejected, lonely or hurt:
so did Jesus. Do we cry out 'Why God, why'? Jesus did the
same.

Since we have been spared the agonies of crucifixion we
should be thankful instead of complaining. There are
some for whom the injunction to take up their cross and
follow Christ is no pious metaphor but an agonising reality. We should be grateful that, as the writer to the
Hebrews says, 'In your struggle against sin, you have not
resisted to the point of shedding your blood' (Hebrews
12:4). That is what love may rightly demand of us. That is
why the world in general will always prefer the politics of
hate. For if there is butchery to be done, love chooses, like
Abel, like Jesus, to be the victim rather than the predator.
Love suffers.

Love shares

'If anyone has material possessions and sees his brother in
need but has no pity on him, how can the love of God be in
him?' (3:17). There is a danger that, in focusing too much
on the extremities that love demands, we can be lulled
into a sense of complacency. We can romanticise about
how we would react if ever we were called upon to play the

role of Sidney Carton, giving ourselves on the guillotine for the salvation of others, and our smug fantasising on the subject blinds us to the fact that there are already many lesser things that we can do for others. They do not amount to martyrdom, but are no less acts of love for being more prosaic and inconspicuous.

John tells us of two things in particular about this sharing. In the first place we must notice his use of the singular: 'If anyone has material possessions and sees his brother...' which is all the more deliberate and striking because of the plural 'brothers' of the preceding verse. Although love is universal in its scope, it may often need to be singular in its application. Love of necessity involves such an intensity of preoccupation with the needs of an individual, that we cannot practise love to all men simultaneously. It is beyond our capacity. Indeed, too wide a protestation of love can simply be a smoke-screen to conceal the superficiality of our real commitment to people.

That is why God is not fooled by our fervent prayers for the starving millions. He is much more concerned about how we respond to that particular case of need next door. This is one of the vital lessons of the Good Samaritan. 'Who is my neighbour?' asked the lawyer, and Jesus replies, 'Your neighbour is that person, of whatever class, tribe or race, that happens to intersect your path. He is your responsibility. He represents love's test for you.'

There is little we can do for those starving millions, though it is easy and cheap to say we love them. But there is no limit to the generosity we might show to that specific individual if we valued him highly enough. Love's sharing then is singular: it focuses on individual needs, not on vague generalised beneficence to the human race.

Secondly, John says that this sharing is practical. 'If anyone has material possessions...' (3:17). Once again, he appears to have the false teaching of the gnostics in mind. You will recall that they were very little interested in men's bodily existence, saying 'The body is evil; it is the spirit that is good,' and as a result gnostic ethics tended to play down the concern for people's material well-being. Almost certainly that is what John is hinting at here, for he is saying that a real Christian would never think like that, and for a very solid theological reason: Jesus came in the flesh and took a human body to heaven.

It follows that real Christian love can never ignore material needs. By becoming flesh, Jesus has elevated the status of our material existence to something of eternal value which we cannot ignore.

'Dear children, let us not love with words or tongue but with actions and in truth.'

'It is the thought that counts', we say. But our complacency is misplaced. Thoughts often count for nothing. Remember James's sarcastic rebuke of the kind of Christian that responds to a brother or sister without clothes or daily food with kind 'thoughts': 'I wish you well, keep warm and well fed.' What good, he says, is that kind of arm-chair philanthropy if it does nothing about the person's physical needs? In the same way John would say that not only is that kind of faith dead, but that kind of love is non-existent. Real love is not only willing to suffer—it is willing to share on a practical and an individual level.

Love goes to heaven

There is a third way in which love contrasts with hate. If hate demonises, love goes to heaven. 'We know that we have passed from death to life, because we love our brothers' (3:14). We must be careful not to misunderstand John here. He is not saying that if we just do works of charity we shall all be certain of heaven in the end. If we read what he is saying in context it is clear that he is talking about Christian love which flows out of a personal commitment to Jesus Christ, and not vague works of charity. Yet what he says is very significant: 'We know that we are heaven bound, because we love.'

What will heaven be like? There is one thing about heaven of which we can be absolutely sure. To use a phrase of Jonathan Edwards', 'Heaven will be a world of love.' It must be so, for God is love.

Again we must not misunderstand what John means by that phrase 'God is love'. God's love does not mean that judgement is an empty threat. John speaks in this verse of an issue of life and death—'We have passed from death to life.' Judgement is dreadfully real, for God is angry with our moral failures. His love does not cancel his righteous anger. That is the whole point of the Cross and of Jesus's coming. Sin matters to God and it is because it matters that there can be no cheap forgiveness. Our sins must be dealt with and they can only be so in two places. Either they are dealt with by Jesus on the cross or they are dealt with in hell. But of one thing we can be sure: God will not overlook sins. There is such a thing as the wrath of God and only a fool ignores it.

Yet the Bible does not say 'God is wrath'. It says 'God is love', for wrath, as Luther puts it, 'is God's strange work'. It is foreign to his essential nature. Wrath is the divine reaction called into existence by the contradictions to his righteous and just character which we human beings perpetrate. It is the provocation of sin that creates God's wrath, and the destruction of that sin quenches that wrath out of existence.

God's wrath is in a very real sense a temporary indignation, but God's love is an eternal energy. Though the Bible tells us there was a time when there was no sin in this world to make God angry, there never was a time when there was no Son in God's heart to make him love. That is the mystery of the Trinity.

Jesus assures us that 'God is love' not just by his atoning sacrifice but by the eternal, divine person he is, and that is why heaven will be a world of love. It cannot be anything else if God is there, and if we are to go to heaven we too must love, says John.

'We know we have passed from death to life, because we love our brothers. Anyone who does not love remains in death' (3:14). God cannot let us into heaven so long as we hate, because we would spoil it. This world was a paradise once, until people like Cain started tearing it apart, and there is no way that God is going to have his new creation ruined by sin in the way the old creation was. So if we would go to heaven, we must lift the word love out of its debased current usage in our sex-obsessed generation, and demonstrate to a world in danger of forgetting what God means by it.

Chapter 7

Confidence

1 John 3:19–24; 4:13–18

If we feel that we lack confidence, there is no shortage of advice for us on the subject. My old piano teacher maintained that it was all a matter of practice. A discreet advertisement in the personal columns of my local newspaper offers it through 'a course of hypnotherapy carried out in the privacy of your own home'. Rodgers & Hammerstein, on the other hand, suggest in a song from their musical *The King and I*, that the secret is to 'whistle a happy tune'; while, according to a well-known TV commercial, it encircles, like a slipped halo, those who are wise enough to use the right toothpaste.

For all that advice, the inferiority complex must be one of the most common neuroses in the self-assertive, success-idolising society in which we live. Whether we contemplate applying for promotion, taking a driving test, engaging a stranger in conversation or whatever, all too often the mere prospect leaves us tongue-tied or leaden-footed.

This world is full of anxiety-ridden individuals who are paralysed from achieving their goals by these and similar demoralising feelings of inadequacy and self-depreciation. It is, of course, possible to be over-confident. We have all met the stuck-up know-it-all who has such an exaggerated opinion of himself that everybody secretly rejoices when

his over-inflated ego suffers a puncture. But to have no
confidence at all is a recipe for disaster in just about every
area of life.

To quote a proverb by Arthur Guiterman:

> He rarely hits the mark,
> Or wins the game,
> Who says, "I know I'll miss,"
> While taking aim.

Ironically, we fail because we think we will fail and so our
defeatism is self-reinforcing. Like a hypochondriac, we
wish weakness upon ourselves when we are in this mood.

It is important to realise that a very similar weakening
syndrome can sap the vigour of the Christian. For confidence is important in our spiritual lives too.

There is undoubtedly such a thing as false assurance,
and the Bible often warns us about it, but the Christian
who is for ever plagued with doubts about his relationship
with God is in some ways no better off. He may not be a
hypocrite, but his joyless example will have little more
impact on his non-Christian environment than if he were.
He may not be a Judas, but the agonies of self-despair and
guilt to which he is inwardly victim will be little less self-
destructive.

While we must avoid presumption and complacency at
all costs, a certain measure of quiet and humble security
in our Christianity is absolutely necessary both to our
usefulness to God and in our enjoyment of him. That is
why 'confidence' is a key word in the Bible. The corresponding Greek word *parrhesia* derived originally from the
political sphere, where it signified the democratic right of
free speech. But, by extension, it gradually came to mean
the kind of candid openness that is not afraid to expose
itself to public gaze. The word is often used in the book of
Acts to describe the fearless way in which the apostles
preached. Here, however, it has much more to do with

personal assurance than evangelism. The word is used in this way, for example, in chapter 3, 'Dear friends, if our hearts do not condemn us, we have *confidence* [*parrhesia*] before God' (3:21), and again in chapter 4, 'Love is made complete among us so that we will have *confidence* on the Day of Judgment' (4:17).

Assurance is, of course, the central and integrating theme of this entire letter and we have already looked at some of the tests by which John tells us a genuine Christian can be authenticated, so that he can be sure that he really is in Christ. But what is a little unexpected is that, according to John, this issue of Christian assurance is also very intimately bound up with the subject of love that we have just been considering. John is drawing the threads of his spiralling thoughts together, and in these closing chapters it becomes more and more obvious that Christian love and Christian confidence are really two sides of the same coin.

Assurance of our salvation

> Dear children, let us not love with words or tongue but with actions and in truth. This then is how we know that we belong to the truth, and how we set our hearts at rest in his presence whenever our hearts condemn us. For God is greater than our hearts, and he knows everything (3:18–20).

This is a passage which commentators delight in, because it is so pregnant with tantalising ambiguity. There are at least half a dozen ways these verses could be legitimately translated. Undoubtedly, the most important issue is the meaning of the phrase in verse 20: 'God is greater than our hearts.' Does John mean that God is greater in the sense that he is likely to be more severe with our failures than we are ourselves? Our hearts, after all, are only aware of a fraction of our sins, but omniscience sees all. So is God's greatness presented as a challenge to us? If our own morally seared consciences give us no peace of heart, what hope can we have of peace before an all holy God? That is a perfectly legitimate way of interpreting the passage, and since no less an exegete than Calvin interpreted it that way, there must be something to be said for it.

On the other hand, does John mean that God is greater in the sense that he is able to be more merciful with our failures than we would be ourselves? While our over-sensitive consciences tend to magnify failure in our minds and obscure the positive and encouraging aspects of our lives, God sees everything in perfect perspective. If that is the right way of understanding it, then God's greatness is a consolation to us, because he is able to overrule our anxious doubts: he knows us better than we know ourselves. This interpretation has been particularly favoured by recent commentators and as it is much more in accord with John's general interest in the letter, I judge it to be the right one.

The American poet and essayist Emerson once wrote, 'Faith is the rejection of lesser fact and the acceptance of a greater fact.' John tells us here that God is the greater fact which we have to accept. We may not be able to forgive ourselves, but it is the verdict of the one who is greater than we are that really counts in the long run.

Three lessons for us

Whichever way we take verse 20, though, mercifully the general lessons of these verses are clear and there are three of them.

The first, according to John, is that it is perfectly normal for genuine Christians to suffer feelings of spiritual uncertainty. Those who are inclined to be anxious or obsessive about things generally will always suffer in this way more than others, but nobody is immune, because nobody is perfect. There are times, as John puts it, when 'our hearts condemn us', and we all know that experience.

The second thing John teaches us is that we must not allow that state of spiritual uncertainty to continue: we should seek a remedy. There are those who regard Christian assurance as essentially presumptuous. Ironically, this is one of the few things that Roman Catholics and hyper-Calvinists have in common. The Roman Catholic can have no assurance because he fears he may fall from grace, the hyper-Calvinist because he is never convinced that he has ever found it. It is plain that they are both wrong: John tells us here that it is possible to have our anxious hearts set at rest in God's presence and to know with certainty that we belong to the truth.

This is, astonishingly, because it is the consequence of the practice of love in our lives: 'Dear children, let us not love with words or tongue but with actions and in truth. This then is how we know that we belong to the truth' (3:18,19). Enshrined in the logic of these two verses, there is both profound psychological truth and a very vital spiritual principle. The psychological truth is that often the reason for our lack of assurance is nothing more than excessive introspection. It is true that we must examine ourselves to see if we are in the faith—the possibility of false assurance demands that—but if we carry it too far, that kind of self-interrogation can be as destructive to our mental balance as the Spanish Inquisition. It is the essence of *agape* love to break us out of this vicious circle of self-absorption and immerse us in self-forgetful involvement with other people.

John puts it to some of us in this way: 'You are lacking confidence in your Christian life because you think about yourself too much. Start putting into practice Christlike living. Is there a brother in need? Then get out and show the love of God to him. Talk less about spiritual things and do more. That is the therapy for these morbid fears you have. Of course you feel depressed while you sit at home and mope! Don't you see, there is an element of self-indulgence in that kind of moroseness and introversion? Get out and love people! Fill your empty hours with Christian action. You will be surprised how quickly self-sacrificial service drives the blues away!' That is the psychological truth that John is hinting at here.

In addition, there is a very vital spiritual principle: that works of love constitute vital objective evidence of the genuineness of our Christian profession.

There was a difference of emphasis on this issue of assurance between the Reformers and the Puritans. The Reformers came very close to taking the line that genuine faith was always accompanied by assurance. Martin Luther suffered terrible torments of conscience, in spite of all his good works and penances, until he discovered the biblical doctrine of justification by faith. Consequently, as a result of his experience of deliverance, anything that suggested that good works could help a Christian was anathema to him. He would tell the fearful Christian to look away from himself to the sufficiency of Christ. The answer to a lack of assurance is a stronger evangelical faith in the grace of God.

The Puritans, however, were very conscious of the way that the doctrine of justification by faith, which Luther taught, had been turned into an excuse for moral licence by some. So they put a great deal more weight upon the importance of observing marks of grace in the believer's life in order to establish assurance. They made sanctification the test of justification, and would tell doubtful Christians to take comfort in the moral evidences of the Holy Spirit's work in their lives.

Ever since the Reformation, there has been a continuing debate among Protestant pastors and theologians about the correct balance between these two approaches to assurance, *objective* assurance based on the work of

Christ on our behalf and *subjective* assurance as we look in and see evidence of Christ changing us.

Undoubtedly, when pushed to extremes, both tend to danger. The Reformers, by emphasising faith, tended to rob more sensitive, less sanguine Christians of that assurance they ought to have had, because they failed to allow for the fact that a weak faith can still be a saving faith. The Puritans, on the other hand, by emphasising self-examination, were in danger of encouraging precisely the kind of self-destructive introspection we discussed earlier.

There is truth, surely, in both camps. Indeed, a careful reading of original literature suggests that the difference between the Reformers and the Puritans may have been rather exaggerated. Yet, in so far as the debate is a real one, I think we have to say, on the basis of 1 John, that the Puritans were undoubtedly right. There is a need for Christians to see their own changed lives as grounds for Christian confidence.

I am fond of the famous soliloquy that John Newton is reputed to have delivered at the breakfast table during family prayers:

> I am not what I ought to be. I am not what I wish to be. I am not what I hope to be. Yet I can truly say, I am not what I once was. By the grace of God I am what I am.

It is only on that kind of candid appraisal of one's life that humble Christian confidence can be built. Indeed, I suspect that the apostle John would refine it further:

"I am not what I ought to be."

"Certainly, you aren't," says John, "for 'if we claim to be without sin, we deceive ourselves.'"

"I am not what I wish to be."

"Certainly not," says John, "for anyone who has the hope

of Christ's return in him, 'purifies himself, just as he is pure'."

"I am not what I hope to be."

"Certainly not," says John, "for 'we know that when he appears, we shall be like him.'"

"Yet I can truly say that I love the brethren, not in mere words but in practical action. That is how I know I belong to the truth and set my heart at rest in his presence whenever my heart condemns me."

Do not misunderstand me: works of love are not the cause of our salvation. I had a relative who was quite convinced that the gates of heaven were going to be flung open to her because she left her estate to the local parish church in her will. She was deluded; we cannot earn salvation by our acts of charity. Salvation is the gift of God in Christ, and it is received by the empty hands of faith.

Yet works of love, says John, are nevertheless an *evidence* of our salvation, and when our guilty hearts rub in the failures and the inadequacies of our lives, it is perfectly proper to answer those accusations. 'We know we have passed from death to life.' Why? 'Because we love our brothers' (3:14). So assurance of salvation is a consequence of practical love, demonstrated in our lives. It turns us outward from ourselves and our morbid broodings and, by furnishing concrete evidence of the work of conversion, it gives a rational answer to our doubting hearts.

Assurance in our praying

'Dear friends, if our hearts do not condemn us, we have confidence before God and receive from him anything we ask, because we obey his commands and do what pleases him' (3:21).

This verse and others like it are a great embarrassment to some folk. Indeed, unanswered prayer is generally a problem to many Christians, arising in two ways. On the one hand, it is an intellectual problem: 'How can we expect prayer to be anything other than unanswered? After all, if God has masterminded the future in advance, prayer has to be redundant.' In Benjamin Disraeli's novel *Lothair*, there is a character called Lord St Aldegonde, who says, 'I am not clear we ought to pray at all. It seems very arrogant in us to dictate to an all-wise Creator what we desire,' and there is a superficial logic in that. At least, like the Moslems, we should surely limit ourselves to prayers of worship and confession. Petitionary prayer must be inconsistent with our doctrine of the sovereignty of God. It suggests that God's will can be changed to our liking.

On the other hand, and perhaps more often, the problem of unanswered prayer is a very practical one. There is some very important issue in our lives: the conversion of someone we love, perhaps, or their healing; deliverance from some situation, habit, or bondage. We pray and pray, but nothing seems to happen. 'Why don't you do anything, God?' we demand. 'Did not Jesus say, "Ask and you will be given"?' This isn't intellectual but practical doubt, born of the failure of experience to corroborate the powerful promises about asking for anything and it being given.

I think that the vital clue to solving both these dilemmas is explicit in what John tells us here. For he says that effective praying is all tied up with the issue of confidence before God: 'If our hearts do not condemn us, we have confidence before God and receive from him anything we ask.' God is not a mechanical blessing dispenser who coughs out the goodies every time we insert the appropriate prayer coin. He is a Father, and he answers our requests in a way analogous to that in which any parent listens to and responds to his children.

To put it another way, prayer is not a technique, but a relationship, and in any relationship mutual confidence is

terribly important. It is in this respect that prayer must be
very carefully distinguished from two other things with
which it is often confused in the popular imagination—
magic and meditation. They are techniques. Magic is a
technique of manipulating supernatural powers to get
what one wants: 'abracadabra', and the rabbit pops out of
the hat. Meditation is a technique for generating an
altered state of consciousness, in which one's own psychic
powers are elevated to a supernatural level: chant 'Hari
Krishna' for five hours and finish up floating to the ceil-
ing.

It is not unusual to find Christians who are unconsciously influenced by occult ideas like these in their attitude to prayer. For instance, I often come across folk who
are convinced that a prayer is not going to be answered
unless it ends with the ritual formula, 'in the name of the
Lord Jesus,' because Jesus' name is a kind of magic incan-
tation for them. Others believe that a prayer is really
going to be answered because of the spiritual fervour of
the one praying; as if prayer was a kind of psychic energy
generated by the human emotion and excitement invested
in it.

It is important that we understand that these are
imported pagan ideas about prayer. Consider the Old
Testament story of the contest on Mount Carmel between
Elijah and the prophets of Baal. The prophet challenged
them to bring down fire on the altar. They chanted and
danced and lacerated themselves in a wild frenzy for hours
on end in an attempt to do so. They were occultists, trying
by means of magic or mystical techniques to get supernatural powers to do something for them. Use the right
formula; perform the right ritual; get yourself 'psyched'
up; that sort of hocus-pocus formed the essence of their
religion.

How different was Elijah. For him there was no exhibitionism; no ecstasy; no spells; no sorcery; just a simple,

rational petition: 'O LORD, God of Abraham, Isaac and Israel, let it be known today that you are God' (1 Kings 18:36). And the fire fell. Elijah's prayer was answered because he had confidence before God. His relationship with God was utterly secure; he knew God's mind; he knew himself to be an instrument of God's purposes; and it was not his will he was seeking to see performed that day, but God's. Indeed, he said as much: 'Let it be known today that you are God in Israel and that I am your servant and have done all these things at your command' (1 Kings 18:36). *That* is confidence.

Jesus made exactly the same point in his teaching about prayer in the Sermon on the Mount. 'When you pray,' he said, 'do not keep on babbling like pagans, for they think they will be heard because of their many words' (Mt 6:7). They think they are going to manipulate God by their incantations. 'Do not be like them, for your Father knows what you need before you ask him' (Mt 6:8).

This is how you should pray: 'Our Father in heaven, hallowed be your name, your kingdom come, your will be done' (Mt 6:9,10). That is prayer; not a technique, but a relationship. It is not a matter of knowing how to get my will done. It is a matter of knowing God well enough to get his will done. So it follows that assurance in prayer lies very much in the intimacy with which we know God and the degree to which our human wills are aligned to his.

John says that 'if our hearts do not condemn us', that is, if we find solid grounds for believing that God really is our Father, then 'we have confidence before God'. Like Elijah, we are confident of God's power and of his purpose. Most important of all, we are confident of our relationship with him, and so 'we receive from him anything we ask', in the same way that children who confidently come to their parents expect them to respond positively to any reasonable and wholesome request, 'because we obey his commands and do what pleases him'. In other words, our prayers are answered because our lives revolve not around our own selfish wills, but around his divine will.

John puts it perhaps even more clearly in chapter 5:

> This is the confidence [*parrhesia*] we have in approaching God: that if we ask anything according to his will, he hears us. And if we know that he hears us—whatever we ask— we know that we have what we asked of him (5:14,15).

So how does prayer achieve anything? A sovereign God cannot change his mind, but nor does he have to. Prayer is about our minds being changed into conformity with his. The humbling and fascinating thing about the God of the Bible is that he feels so strongly about the Father-son relationship he wants to have with us that he actually organises the way he runs the universe so as to perform his will in response to our prayers. I am in no doubt that, if he so wanted, he could run the whole show without any assistance from us at all. We could just be relegated to the role of passive spectators in every respect. But he does not want to do it like that. He wants to build a kingdom where men and women, who have surrendered to his sovereign rule over their lives, consciously energise that will in the world and prayer is one way in which we can do that. It is part of the work he gives us to do, one of the means whereby we obtain what he is all too willing to give.

What, then, about unanswered prayer—the things we have asked for so often and not received? One explana- tion, the Bible tells us, is that we may be asking amiss. That is why it is important to note the phrase, 'if we ask anything according to his will'. Prayer is not a blank cheque that God is pledged to sign whatever we write on the dotted line. If that is what we want, it is not prayer we are after, but magic. Prayer is only effective in so far as it reflects an obedient heart submissive to God's will.

We would never expect loving parents to give their children literally anything they asked for. Jesus said,

'Which of you, if his son asks for bread, will give him a stone?...how much more will your Father in heaven give good gifts to those who ask him!' (Mt 7:9,11). But what if a child is foolish enough to ask for a stone, what does the Father do then? We do not always know what is best for us, and faith sometimes means accepting that God's wisdom is superior to ours in that respect.

The apostle Paul besought God to deliver him from some painful physical trial a number of times, but God said, 'My grace is sufficient for you' (2 Cor 12:9). Similarly, Jesus prayed in Gethsemane: 'Father, if it is possible, may this cup be taken from me.' Even his prayer, you see, was conditional upon God's will. That is why he continued: 'Yet not as I will, but as you will' (Mt 26:39).

It is possible, then, that our prayer is unwise and God is overruling it because he has a better purpose in mind.

Alternatively, if our prayers are unanswered, it may be because God is delaying his answer. There are several occasions in the Bible when we find people had to wrestle with God to obtain the blessing they sought. Moses' forty days on the mountain is a good example of that. Why did God not give him what he wanted on the first day—it would have saved a lot of time? Another example from the Old Testament is Jacob's wrestling with the angel. I suspect that, often, the reason for such delay is that God does not want us to take his generosity for granted. After all, if a parent accedes to the request of his child hastily, it may breed a spoiled presumptuousness. He may be willing all the time to give, but his wisdom makes him wait, so that when he does grant the request, it is accompanied by deep gratitude, not smug self-satisfaction.

God may deal with us in the same way in answering our prayers, delaying to test our persistence not because he is reluctant and needs to be persuaded, but because we need to be more deeply conscious of his grace before it is safe for us to be blessed as we desire. Certainly there are many parables in the Gospels in which Jesus exhorts us not to give up praying just because an answer is not immediately forthcoming.

If we are not asking amiss and if God is not delaying in his answer, a further possible reason for our prayers remaining unanswered is that we do not yet enjoy the confidence before God which John is speaking about. Our relationship with God is too distant. After all, God is in no way obliged to answer the prayers of unbelievers. Sometimes he does, but not because he has any fatherly commitment to do so. If our relationship is distant from him and insecure, if perhaps some sin comes between us or some lack of personal assurance is weakening our relationship with him, it may very well be that, to chasten us, to teach us or to draw us back to himself, our prayers will not be answered as we would wish them to be.

'If I had cherished sin in my heart,' says the Psalmist, 'the Lord would not have listened' (Ps 66:18). He is not saying that we have to be perfect before our prayers are answered, but that the consciousness of unforgiven sin destroys our confidence in prayer, as indeed it must. Peter is probably making much the same point when he comments in 1 Peter chapter 3 that an unresolved row between husband and wife can hinder their prayers. If we are not loving as we should be, then we cannot point to any evidence in our lives that we are God's children. Similarly, if 'our hearts condemn us' in that way, we can have no confidence in our access into God's presence and no certainty that God will hear us. How can we exercise faith that he will answer our requests, if we are not even sure that we have any right to expect him to hear us?

Assurance in prayer, John is telling us here, is one of the privileges of being assured of our salvation. The one rests upon the other, and both rest ultimately upon the practice of love in our lives. Jesus implied that when, having said, 'The Father will give you whatever you ask in my name,' straight away added, 'This is my command: Love each other' (Jn 15:16,17).

Assurance in our experience

> No one has ever seen God, but if we love one another, God lives in us and his love is made complete in us. We know that we live in him and he in us, because he has given us of his Spirit (4:12,13).

Experience is vital to Christianity, indeed there cannot be any without it. I should certainly never want to run it down. One of the things John is trying to do in this epistle is to undermine the prominence given by the gnostic heretics to mystical experience. To him, the desire to have direct, sensual contact with God, to feel God in private devotional ecstasy and the whole theology which the gnostics built upon that, is misguided. But John never says that experience of God is invalid. How could it be? The prophets and saints of every age have testified to great spiritual elevations, when they have felt God's presence in quite remarkable ways. Most of us, I expect, can remember occasions in our experience when we were lifted, if not quite with Paul up to the third heaven, at least to the first or second! Those are precious times and God forbid that anyone should think John or I want to rob people of that 'inexpressible and glorious joy', but there is an important balance to be maintained in this matter. Today, as in John's day, there are many who are leaning far too far in the gnostic direction of obsession with such mystical ecstatic experience.

Tragically, it is all tied up with the Holy Spirit. I use such a word deliberately, because it is the Holy Spirit who above every other person is concerned with the unity of the church. So it is bitterly ironic that the doctrine of the Holy Spirit should in our day become an issue of division, but it has, there is no point in pretending otherwise. The question about Christian experience debated today is, 'What does it mean to have an experience of the Holy Spirit and how can I know that I have enjoyed it?'

At the risk of again being misunderstood, I want to make some observations on that from what John says in these verses. Notice first of all, that, according to John, the gift of the Holy Spirit is an inevitable corollary of our union with Christ: 'We know that we live in him and he in us, because he has given us of his Spirit' (4:13). The Spirit is a test. There is no room here for a true Christian without the Spirit. If we have not received the Holy Spirit, we are not in Christ.

John makes absolutely no mention of any mystical experiences as signs or evidences of our receiving the Spirit. That isn't what he is talking about, as we have already endeavoured to prove. There are those, of course, who will suggest that the reception of the Holy Spirit is always accompanied by profound emotional disturbances. Some put forward the view that speaking in tongues is a concomitant of the experience of the Holy Spirit. I suggest that, if it were so that a person who has received the Holy Spirit must necessarily speak in tongues, it is inconceivable that John should not have referred to it, because the whole purpose of his letter is to reassure doubting Christians and provide them with criteria by which they should know that they are really saved. If an unmistakable evidence of the gift of the Holy Spirit is that we speak in tongues, surely John would have included it in his list of criteria by which an authentic Christian can be distinguished. But he does not do this, and for two very good reasons.

First of all, I suspect that he makes no mention of it because the majority of Christians did not speak in tongues in his day, any more than they do now. There is no New Testament evidence that they did.

Secondly, and more importantly, he is silent on the point because, in John's day, ecstatic utterances were the distinguishing mark, not of orthodox believers but of the gnostic heretics he was seeking to refute. They were the ones who were in favour of the prophetic gift and new revelations in the church.

Another thing we must notice from what John says here is that the experience of the Holy Spirit is not mystical in nature. Its consequences, he says, are confessional and moral. There is a paradox here:

> We know that we live in him and he in us, because he has given us of his Spirit (4:13).
>
> If anyone acknowledges that Jesus is the Son of God, God lives in him and he in God (4:15).
>
> Whoever lives in love lives in God, and God in him (4:16).

The same points are also made at the end of chapter 3:

> This is his command: to believe in the name of his Son, Jesus Christ, and to love one another as he commanded us. Those who obey his commands live in him, and he in them. And this is how we know that he lives in us: we know it by the Spirit he gave us (3:23,24).

This, then, is Christian experience. To John, to live in God and to have God living in us is not primarily a description of some ecstatic or emotional experience. While there may be emotion attached to it, he is not primarily talking about that but about our Christian faith and practice. Of course, this does not mean that mystical feelings are not a valid part of Christian experience, because they certainly are, but as far as assurance goes, they are relatively unimportant.

I do not believe anybody is better qualified to talk about this subject than Jonathan Edwards, who personally witnessed a remarkable series of revivals in New England in the eighteenth century. As is often the case, those events were accompanied by some remarkable exhibitions of spiritual emotion. Quite a number of conservative churchmen in Edwards' day were deeply suspicious of these outbursts of 'religious hysteria', as they termed it, for, in those rationalistic days, emotions were supposed to be kept well out of public display. As a result, Jonathan Edwards wrote a book entitled *A Treatise on the Religious Affections*[8] in which he seeks to defend biblically and theologically the place of emotion and affection in the Christian life, and does so extremely convincingly.

It is a classic study and a very important book in the current climate of charismatic controversy. But it is very important to notice one thing: Jonathan Edwards is very concerned not to overstate the importance of religious affection. It is no necessary sign of grace, he says, that religious affections are very great and raised very high; or that people are disposed to praise and glorify God.

Jonathan Edwards had gone through revival and knew enough about religious emotionalism to be aware that feelings can be very misleading. He insisted that true and gracious religious affections differ from that which is false in that (i) they are attended by a conviction of the reality and certainty of divine truth—in other words, they result in an orthodox Christian confession; (ii) they beget and promote a spirit of love and meekness—that is, they are accompanied by Christian character; (iii) supremely, gracious and holy affections have their exercise and root in Christian practice. That is the point he makes over and over again in the final chapter of the book. What we do as Christians is the distinguishing and sure evidence of grace to our neighbours and also to our own conscience. We are not to judge our spiritual state by inward spiritual experiences. Such things are all too easily counterfeited by Satan, and their intensity is altogether too much influenced by our personality and temperament. Rather, Christian practice is the only sure and reliable test.

If we want to know whether or not we have experienced the Holy Spirit, we do not have to ask ourselves if we have spoken in tongues or if we have felt overwhelmed with spiritual emotion. These things may indeed be true or

they may not, but they prove nothing one way or another.
Rather, we have to ask ourselves if we have a conviction
that Jesus is the Son of God and a sincere desire to
respond to his love by loving others. If that is our life's
ambition, then we have an experience of the Holy Spirit.

That is the way he manifests himself in people's lives.
And that is why I am personally convinced the charismatic movement generally speaking is a genuine movement of Christian renewal and not a gnostic heresy. Not
because they have tongues and healings and dancing
down the aisles; the charismatics are a manifestation of
genuine Christian revival because they are orthodox in
their view of Jesus and they practise love. Indeed, they are
an example to us all in the way they defend the authority
of Jesus and demonstrate practical care to one another.

Christian experience is not about whipping up emotional ecstasy, but about facing up to a conviction that
Jesus is God and demonstrating the love of God in our
practical living. If emotion comes, praise God. If it
doesn't, praise him still. It makes no real difference, for
assurance is a consequence of *agape* love, rooted you will
remember, not in the emotions, but in the mind and the
will.

And those who enjoy such assurance need have no fear
of the future. They can even anticipate the Day of Judgement, not in trembling anxiety but quiet *confidence*.

> Love is made complete among us so that we will have
> confidence on the Day of Judgment, because in this world
> we are like him. There is no fear in love. But perfect love
> drives out fear, because fear has to do with punishment.
> The one who fears is not made perfect in love (4:17,18).

Chapter 8

Faith

1 John 5:1–21

John has instructed us about many things regarding Christian experience in this letter. He has taught the importance of moral conduct, because anybody who claims to know God but does not obey his commandments is a liar. He has taught the importance, too, of sound doctrine, because if anybody denies that Jesus is the Christ, who came in the flesh, such a one is the Antichrist. Practical love is also vital, because if anybody hates his brother, he is a murderer. Yet although conduct, doctrine and love are all vital components of Christian living, John somehow managed, with masterly self-restraint, to leave the primary and fundamental characteristic of Christianity to the very last: 'Who is it that overcomes the world? Only he who believes that Jesus is the Son of God' (5:5).

I suppose it is inevitable that preachers and expositors always think that the particular study they are engaged in at the moment is especially important. Yet when I say that the subject we are going to examine in this last chapter is not just weighty but crucial, I want you to believe me. For, important as moral conduct is, the Bible does not say we are saved by conduct. Vital as orthodoxy is, the Bible never says we are saved by that either. Nor

137

does it ever say that we are saved by *agape*—love. What it does say repeatedly is that we are saved by faith, and that is what we are going to consider now. It is a matter that none of us can afford to neglect, for it concerns our destiny. There is no issue of greater consequence than the question of whether or not we are believers.

The focus of faith

'This is the one who came by water and blood—Jesus Christ. He did not come by water only, but by water and blood' (5:6).

By any standards, 'by water and blood' is a cryptic phrase and scholars have occupied pages of their learned commentaries in discussing its meaning. One theory is that water and blood are references to Jesus' death on the cross. The grounds for this is a verse in the Gospel of John, where we read: 'One of the soldiers pierced Jesus' side with a spear, bringing a sudden flow of blood and water' (Jn 19:34). It is clear that John did see a special significance in that, because he draws attention to it in the Gospel, adding, 'The man who saw it has given testimony, and his testimony is true.' So it is likely there is some kind of connection between blood and water in John chapter 19 and blood and water here in 1 John chapter 5. But there must be more to it because if blood and water simply means the death of Jesus, it does not really furnish any clear explanation of why John should add this mysterious phrase.

A second theory which is very popular is that water and blood in this chapter refer to the two sacraments of the Christian church, baptism and holy communion. Again, it is very likely that to a first-century ear the words, water and blood, would prompt such thoughts, but that interpretation does not explain the significance of the rather clumsy expression that Jesus Christ *came* by water and blood, either. In what way are baptism and communion the instruments of Jesus' mission?

As is so often the case in regard to these ambiguous expressions of John, the clue lies in the false teaching of the gnostics he was writing to refute. In the first chapter of this book, we mentioned the gnostic heretic Cerinthus with whom, according to tradition, the apostle John had an altercation in the Ephesian public baths. Cerinthus taught that the Christ was a divine spirit that descended on the man Jesus at his baptism in Jordan. He denied the true Incarnation and that, we noticed, was why John was so emphatic that anybody who will not acknowledge that Jesus Christ has come in the flesh is of the Antichrist.

That error was bad enough, but in fact Cerinthus did not stop there. He went on to argue that, since spirits at least in the Greek mind could not suffer, whatever divinity Jesus had must have departed from him before the cross. Consequently, the person who died on Calvary was not 'the Christ', because 'the Christ' had gone back to heaven long before. The person who suffered on the cross was just an ordinary Galilean peasant, Jesus, who had for a time provided 'the Christ' with bodily accommodation. What is more, there is evidence, albeit slight, that some gnostic groups in this tradition in the early second century absented themselves from communion in church, precisely because the limited Christ in whom they believed did not die. Though they practised baptism, the Lord's Supper was a meaningless event for them.

Now we can begin to see what John is getting at when he says, 'He did not come by water only, but by water and blood.' As so often in John's writing, the ambiguity is intentional, and all the lines of rival interpretation probably have elements of truth in them. The blood and the water that flowed from Jesus' side on the cross were significant in John's mind, precisely because he was writing against the background of gnostic controversy. He saw a kind of divine sign against the gnostic in that rather gory observation that water and blood were both there in the cross. Baptism and Communion were equally important to him, because they witnessed to the two extremities of Jesus' earthly ministry which the gnostics were trying to truncate. But the vital and central point he is trying to make here is about faith.

Authentic faith, he says, lays hold of a complete Jesus, whose mission started in Jordan with the descent of the Holy Spirit, but was not culminated until Calvary. The religion of Cerinthus was one of enlightenment, focusing on an experience of mystical union with God. But John's was one of faith focused on an act of substitutionary atonement by God. 'He did not come by water only, but by water and blood.'

There is a way in which this attitude of Cerinthus which John is combating here is still with us today. Consider how many people are very willing to sentimentalise about the Christmas story, though they have very little interest at all in Easter. A God who comes to us as a baby in a stable is an attractive proposition, but a God who hangs before us, naked, agonised, bloody, we would prefer not to think about. Yet John is saying here that if our faith in Jesus is genuine, it must be one which embraces the cross as well as the manger, the blood as well as the water.

One person who understood this very well was the Christian poet, William Cowper. He wrote a hymn which I have to confess I find very difficult to sing congregationally, because it is full of such gory imagery that I am always frightened it may offend someone or, worse still, be cheapened by the thoughtlessness with which we so often sing sacred poetry. Yet if we want to know the true focus of Christian faith, we can do little better than meditate on its words:

There is a fountain filled with blood,
Drawn from Immanuel's veins;
And sinners plunged beneath that flood
Lose all their guilty stains.

Ee'r since, by faith, I saw the stream
Thy flowing wounds supply,
Redeeming love has been my theme,
And shall be till I die.[9]

That is the focus of a true faith: a Jesus who comes not
'by water only, but by water and blood', a Jesus who not
only lives the life of God, but who shed the blood of God.

The source of faith

John continues: 'And it is the Spirit who testifies, because
the Spirit is the truth' (5:6).

It is often suggested that the fundamental reason people
do not believe the preaching of the gospel is lack of proof.
Rationalism runs deep in the veins of twentieth-century
thought and non-Christians are never slow in mustering
its intellectual armoury in defence of their scepticism.
Faith, they proclaim, is an illogical belief in the improb-
able; a mystification of Freudian parental dependencies;
an act of wishful thinking. In principle, there is nothing to
choose between believing in Jesus and believing in fairies
at the bottom of the garden. Faith, as the little boy wrote
in his school essay, 'is believing what you know is not
true'.

'Prove it to me and then I'll believe.' But is that an
honest objection? I have a deep suspicion that in the vast
majority of cases all this demand for proof is at best a
smoke screen and at worst a red herring. It is a smoke
screen because behind it the unbeliever can hide the fact
that the gospel, for all the intellectual holes he thinks he
can pick in it, has a strange ability to disturb his conscience and puncture his security. It is a red herring

because it so easily seduces the naïve Christian into arguing his faith on the false humanistic premise of his rivals, rather than attacking those presuppositions themselves. For the fact is that authentic faith has very little interest in proof.

Faith, properly understood, is not a conclusion reached at the end of a chain of deductive reasoning, or scientific evidence, but, as John makes clear here, it is primarily a Spirit-given intuition. It is not that I struggle to convince myself of things I know to be highly dubious. Rather, I surrender to things which, by divine illumination, I now inwardly perceive to be glaringly self-evident. 'It is the Spirit who testifies, because the Spirit is the truth.'

Anselm and Aquinas

Down through history the profoundest Christian thinkers have always understood this and distinguished themselves from more shallow theologians by it. Anselm, the great eleventh-century theologian, for example, states this quite clearly in his book *Proslogion* in words that have since become quite famous: '*Credo ut intelligam*'—'I believe in order to understand.' The function of reason, he argues in that book, is not to create faith, nor even to justify it, but to understand it.

In that, Anselm contrasts markedly with the later medieval scholastic, Thomas Aquinas, a much more superficial theologian who, in my view quite disastrously, sought to fuse Christian theology with Greek rationalism. He introduced the idea of offering proofs of God's existence by philosophical argument, trying to create what he called a natural theology—that is, based on reason rather than revelation. And it was the demolition of those classical proofs of God's existence by Kant in the eighteenth century that must be regarded as one of the major causes of the rise of modern atheism. That was a tragedy, if ever

there was one, because the more virile theology of Anselm
would never have sought to build itself upon such a vulnerable, rationalistic foundation.

Descartes and Pascal

A more recent contrast can be found between René
Descartes and Blaise Pascal in the seventeenth century.
Descartes, like Aquinas, was a rationalist, and the Cartesian philosophy he founded rests all certainty on scientific
verification. As a consequence, the only grounds
Descartes could find for sustaining his own religious faith
was the authority of the church, which of course inevitably
collapsed and contributed further in the following centuries to the growth of atheistic humanism.

Pascal, on the other hand, with a more sure grasp of the
nature of religious conviction, says in his *Pensées*: 'This is
faith, God felt by the heart not by the reason. The heart
has its reasons which reason cannot know.' We must not
be misled by Pascal's use of the word 'heart' into thinking
that he is a sentimentalist, for by it he means what we
would call intuition, as he makes quite clear in a longer
passage where he speaks directly against the Cartesian
approach. He argues that the knowledge of primary principles, like space, time, motion and number, is not
attained by reasoning, but reason must trust the intuitions
of the heart and base her every argument upon them. It is
useless and absurd for reason to demand from the heart
proofs of her first principles.

Pascal goes on to say that this inability ought to humble
reason, so we should not wonder to see simple people
believing without reasoning, for God imparts to them love
of him. He inclines their hearts to believe. Men will never
believe with a saving and real faith, unless God inclines
their hearts, and they will believe as soon as he so inclines
it. If one remembers that he was a Roman Catholic, that is

a remarkable piece of Calvinistic theology! It is, in fact, the identical argument which is put by the Puritan John Owen at much greater length, in his major work, *The Reason of Faith*.

It is important that we do not misunderstand Anselm, Pascal, Owen or the apostle John at this point. They are not saying that faith is implicitly irrational, or that there is no value in Christian apologetics. The whole point about Christianity is that, unlike mystical Gnosticism, it is anchored in concrete, objective facts of history which are sufficiently well accredited by eye-witnesses to make the Christian faith a perfectly reasonable one. That is probably what John means when he says: 'There are three that testify: the Spirit, the water and the blood; and the three are in agreement' (5:7,8). Water and blood, as we have just seen, are shorthand for the historical dimension of Jesus' existence to which the apostles testify. Maybe there is also an allusion to the on-going proclamation of those gospel facts through the ordinances of baptism and the Lord's Supper in the life of the church. Either way, the water and the blood stand for the objective elements of the Christian faith.

The apostles did not, like the gnostics, come to the world offering just an experience. They came testifying to an event, to good news, something that had happened. The water and the blood; Jesus the Son of God anointed by the Spirit, dying for men's sins; they were eye-witnesses of these things. That is why in the book of Acts you find the apostles reasoning with their audiences in attempts to persuade them of the truth of the gospel. 'What I am saying is true and reasonable,' Paul told Festus. 'It was not done in a corner' (Acts 26:25,26). Failure to preach the gospel in that mind-orientated way inevitably invites the charge that conversion is just an emotional experience, which it emphatically is not.

My own training as a natural scientist means that I
could never be a believer unless I was persuaded that that
in which I was putting my faith was really true, not just
subjectively, but true out there in the real world, irrespective of whether I believe in it or not; or, to put it another
way, objectively true.

Pascal and those who agree with him are not saying
that Christianity is just a subjective experience. But they
insist that even if all the evidence and the argument of
2,000 years of Christian apologetics were mustered, it
would not amount to proof. For faith is not ultimately a
logical inference but a Spirit-given intuition: 'It is the
Spirit who testifies, because the Spirit is the truth' (5:6).
There is nothing unusual or unwarranted about that says
John. 'We accept man's testimony, but God's testimony is
greater' (5:9). It is common human experience to trust
other people. We use our intuition about people and say,
'Yes, I think I can trust him.' When we ask someone the
way and that person gives the impression of being reliable,
we act on their guidance. We cannot prove it. In a very
real sense the only proof available lies in the going and in
the eventual arriving. But we all recognise that testimony
is a credible ground for practical faith. How much more
sufficient, John teaches us here, is God's testimony by his
Spirit: 'Anyone who believes in the Son of God has this
testimony in his heart.... And this is the testimony: God
has given us eternal life, and this life is in his Son'
(5:10,11). As Pascal said, 'The heart has its reasons, which
reason cannot know.'

To use an analogy, faith is not like wrestling with a
geometric theory till we arrive at the end and say, 'There,
I worked it out, there is the proof.' Faith is much more like
having cataracts taken off one's eyes. Sometimes it is just
as sudden as that too. 'I can see it,' we say. 'Why couldn't
I see it before? I must have been blind.' That is why in
earlier times people used to talk about seeing the light,

which expresses in a very real sense what authentic faith feels like. It arrives not in the context of self-congratulation—'my! how clever I am!'—but as an experience of divine revelation. So, when Peter first confessed Jesus, 'You are the Christ, the Son of the living God,' Jesus did not say, 'Well done, Peter. You did well to arrive at that conclusion,' but, 'Blessed are you, Simon son of Jonah, for this was not revealed to you by man, but by my Father in heaven' (Mt 16:16,17).

To take the line of Aquinas and Descartes and offer people proof is to imply that that proof is available and thus not to promote faith at all. In the long term it is to promote atheism. To quote the apostle Paul, 'For since in the wisdom of God the world through its wisdom did not know him, God was pleased through the foolishness of what was preached to save those who believe' (1 Cor 1:21).

Vital as faith is to John's interest in this book, we look in vain in this chapter or in the whole letter for rationalistic arguments to bolster up his readers' confidence. There is no philosophical discussion of the ontological proof of God's existence. There is no scholarly treatise on the historical reliability of the Gospels, not even a brief rundown of the evidence for the Resurrection. John does not argue for faith, he simply assumes it will be there in any true Christian experience, as chapter 5 verse 1 tells us: 'Everyone who believes that Jesus is the Christ is born of God.' Faith is not self-manufactured; it is evidence of the fact that God has taken a supernatural initiative in a person's life, that he is born of God. Notice the tenses: he 'who believes' (present tense), 'is born' (past tense). If we must talk about an order of salvation, this is it: we are not born of God as a consequence of our faith; we believe as a consequence of our new birth. To use again the vocabulary of Paul, faith is not a human 'work', lest we should boast about it: faith is 'the gift of God' (Eph 2:8–9).

It is vital that we understand this if we are not to be frustrated about this matter of faith. Faith does not ultimately rest on human reason and argument. If it did, of course, the intellectuals would have the advantage. No, faith rests on the inner testimony of the Holy Spirit, an intuition of the heart supported, defended, understood by our minds, and so not contrary to our reasoning process, but nevertheless a God-given intuition.

I cannot do better than quote a paragraph from a book by Frederick Buechner, *The Magnificent Defeat*, where he talks about it:

> In our twentieth century, we all want to be certain, we all want proof, but the kind of proof we tend to want— scientifically and philosophically demonstrable proof that would silence all doubts once and for all—would not in the long run, I think, answer the fearful depths of our need at all. For what we need to know is not just that God exists, but that there is a God right here in the thick of our day-to-day lives as we move around knee-deep in the fragrant muck and misery and marvel of this world. It is not objective proof of God's existence we want, but the experience of God's presence. That is the miracle we are really after—and that also, I think, is the miracle we really get.[10]

The fruit of faith

'For everyone born of God overcomes the world. This is the victory that has overcome the world, even our faith' (5:4).

Once a person understands that the focus of Christian faith is Jesus who died and that the source of that faith is the inner conviction of the Holy Spirit, there is a further obstacle that may hinder him, and that is the fear that he will not be able to handle the changes involved if he does believe. It is no good minimising those changes, since they are considerable. John has repeatedly emphasised in this letter that we can have no relationship with a holy God without a correspondingly holy life style. And he reiterates that in verse 3: 'This is love for God: to obey his commands.' When we read our Bibles carefully, we discover that those commands embrace every area of life. Attitude to money, our career ambitions, our sexual behaviour, our personal decision making in just about every sphere must be brought under critical review and assessed by the standards of God's rule book if we are to become Christians. The changes demanded can be very costly and I can sympathise with anyone who sincerely aspires to Christian commitment, but is genuinely not sure that he wants to face the implications of such radical obedience.

After all, it is not as if our secular environment is conducive to a Christian life style. Our family, perhaps, will be hostile to us. Maybe our old friends will jeer at us. The mass media surrounds us, all dedicated to seducing us morally and intellectually from the way of holiness. Our entire culture, it seems increasingly today, is antagonistic to Christian values. What hope have we of living successfully as Christians in obedience to God's command with the pressure of the world against us? At the very best surely our Christian lives are going to be ones of unceasing struggle and failure. Is it worth it? There is, after all, always that sneaking suspicion that God is a sadistic killjoy anyway. Perhaps he wants to spoil our fun. He does seem to have a penchant for prohibiting many activities which non-Christians seem to have a good time doing.

John answers such hesitations. God's moral requirements are not onerous. The secular environment need not deter us. The answer to both these things is the fruit of faith: victory. 'This is the victory that has overcome the world, even our faith' (5:4).

There is something we must understand about Christian faith: it creates a bond between the believer and

Jesus. Faith in and of itself is weak and helpless. Placed in any other object, it would achieve nothing. But when a person believes in Jesus, things start happening in his life of which in and of himself he would have been quite incapable. It is a bit like the rope that connects the water skier to the launch. When a person is linked by faith to Christ, a power is unleashed in his life for holiness and witness. Changes come. I do not say there is no struggle in those changes, no pain to endure, no problems to solve or no cross to bear. Jesus said there would be. This triumph of which John speaks is not without its cost, but it is a certain triumph, one for which the Christian fights, not in grudging sullenness, but with a taste of glory in his mouth. The campaign may be long and sometimes gruelling, but the end cannot be in doubt. For, as John has said earlier, 'You, dear children, are from God and have overcome them, because the one who is in you is greater than the one who is in the world' (4:4). This is the victory that has overcome the world: our faith.

A question

John closes his letter with a challenge to every one of us to faith. He challenges the non-Christian by stating the sobering consequences of a failure to believe. 'Anyone who does not believe God has made him out to be a liar, because he has not believed the testimony God has given about his Son' (5:10). Make no mistake about it, unbelief is a sin, for it is a defamation of God's person. It is a slander against his veracity, and according to John, the punishment for that sin is death: 'He who has the Son has life; he who does not have the Son of God does not have life' (5:12).

He challenges the back-slider, too: 'If anyone sees his brother commit a sin that does not lead to death, he should pray and God will give him life' (5:16). Perhaps we made a profession of faith in Christ some time ago, but our commitment has grown so weak that we have lost a sense of God's presence in our life and moral rebellion is re-asserting its presence in our experience. John's warning in this verse is very clear, we dare not be complacent about our state if we are back-sliders. We can have no more assurance of eternal life in a state of back-sliding than a person who has never responded to Christ at all. If that is our situation, John says that we must find a Christian brother or sister and ask him or her to pray with us and for us. Our condition is not impossible, it can be remedied. Spiritual life can be restored in our experience, 'God will give him life.' But beware because if that life is not restored in us, then our soul may harden into a condition of irreversible apostasy, like that of Judas, for which God will accept no intercession and from which no repentance is psychologically possible. 'There is a sin that leads to death' (5:16). We need to heed the words of John, to repent and seek the pardon and renewal of God while we have the opportunity.

John challenges believers here as well: 'I write these things to you who believe in the name of the Son of God so that you may know...' (5:13). Maybe we have been feeling under attack like these Christians to whom John is writing. Perhaps there are super-spiritual groups like the gnostics around that make us feel inadequate. Then, we must learn, says John, to rest upon the certainties of faith: 'We know that anyone born of God does not continue to sin; the one who was born of God keeps him safe, and the Evil One cannot harm him' (5:18). Conduct, then, is the only sure evidence of conversion. We must not let anyone deceive us with the thought that there is something else which we need in order to confirm faith to our hearts.

'We know that we are the children of God, and that the whole world is under the control of the Evil One' (5:19). So we must expect anti-Christian opposition, and temptation. Both are inevitable in a fallen world, but we must not let such things demoralise us.

> We know also that the Son of God has come and has given us understanding, so that we may know him who is true. And we are in him who is true—even in his Son Jesus Christ. He is the true God and eternal life (5:20).

So in Christ we have come face to face with the ultimate truths of the universe. By faith we have embraced the ultimate, the absolute truth for which many philosophers and scientists are searching. However, it does not lie in any equation or syllogism, but in a person. The Son of God has come and given us an understanding that we may know him who is truth. He is the one who holds the universe together and who will bring history to its climax. We know him. Let us persevere in those certainties.

'Dear children, keep yourself from idols' (5:21). John warns us not to prostitute our faith on unworthy objects of human speculation and opinion. The focus of our faith is Jesus. He is the true God and eternal life. The source of our faith is the Holy Spirit's testimony in our heart, and the fruit of that faith, we will discover, is victory over the world.

Are we ready for faith?

Notes

1   John R W Stott *Your Mind Matters* (IVP 1972).
2   Joseph Fletcher *Situation Ethics* (Westminster Press, Philadelphia 1966).
3   John Alexander Joyce, d 1915 *There are no pockets in a shroud.*
4   John Hick (ed) *The Myth of God Incarnate* (SCM Press Ltd, London, 1977)
5   H Twells 'At even ere the sun was set' *Hymns Ancient and Modern Revised* (William Clowes & Sons Ltd, London, 1972)
6   John R W Stott *Epistles of John* (IVP 1983).
7   St Augustine *Confessions* 8:9
8   Jonathan Edwards *Religious Affections* (Yale Univ. Press, 1959).
9   William Cowper 'There is a fountain filled with blood' *Hymns of Faith* (Scripture Union, London, 1982).
10 Frederick Buechner *The Magnificent Defeat* (Seabury Press, New York 1966).

Introducing Jesus

by Roy Clements

Large format paperback

People's lives fascinate us. Today more than ever we consume articles and watch chat shows, all to learn from a safe distance as much as we can about the joys and griefs of others.

Jesus had his admirers and onlookers too. But he remained a mystery to those who were not prepared to meet the man behind the image.

Through skilful exposition and challenging argument Roy Clements gives us an opportunity to get to know the real Jesus, as he takes us through a series of conversations and discourses reported in John's Gospel. He does not stop there, but goes on to relate the Bible's teaching to the beliefs and opinions of contemporary man. However you view the claims of Jesus, you will be left in no doubt that, correctly understood, they are of profound relevance to our lives even in this nuclear age.

'Some readers will surely be brought by the Holy Spirit to faith in Jesus. Others will have their faith clarified and strengthened. None of us can fail to be enriched.'

—From the Foreword by John Stott

'Brilliant, crisp, incisive and compelling.'

—Sir Fred Catherwood, MEP

'A book to set the soul on fire.'

—David Porter, writer and editor

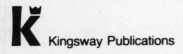

Kingsway Publications

Chosen for Good

**by Peter Lewis, Roy Clements and
Greg Haslam**

Edited by Robert Horn

Three men, endowed with a remarkable gift of teaching,
expound the basics of the Christian gospel. Here we see
man in his need, in utter degradation and hopelessness.
Yet we also see God in his glory, choosing to bring lost
men and women back into the light of his presence and
showering on them the blessings of eternal life.

In this book we learn—

   — how God sees mankind today
   — what he has decided to do about man's plight
   — the meaning of Christ's death on the cross
   — how we can believe the gospel
   — how we can know God will never let us go

The authors guide us carefully through the theological
minefield that has been laid around these great truths,
and helpfully apply them to our everyday lives. As such
it is ideal not only for new Christians, but for all those
who wish to gain a deeper appreciation of what God has
done for us in Christ.

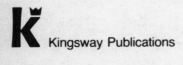

Kingsway Publications

The Gift of Prophecy

by Wayne Grudem

If the Bible is the word of God, and nothing more can be added to its pages, why should we need the gift of prophecy?

If prophecy is speaking words inspired by God, has Scripture ceased to be our only ultimate authority?

These two questions represent the confusion and anxiety felt by many Christians today. In response, Wayne Grudem gives a masterly presentation of the nature and role of prophecy. In so doing he points the way to a new understanding that preserves the uniqueness of Scripture while allowing the church room to enjoy one of God's most edifying gifts.

'It should be read by charismatics and non-charismatics alike. They will find that they are closer together than they thought.'
—Peter Lewis, Pastor,
Cornerstone Evangelical Church, Nottingham

'The discovery of Wayne's thesis radically transformed my understanding of prophecy in the New Testament.'
—Roy Clements, Pastor, Eden Baptist Chapel, Cambridge

'An important contribution to the study of prophecy in the early church.'
—FF Bruce

WAYNE GRUDEM was educated at Westminster Theological Seminary, and Harvard and Cambridge Universities. He is Associate Professor of Systematic Theology at Trinity Evangelical Divinity School near Chicago.

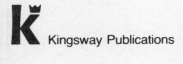

Kingsway Publications